Introduction to Computer Programming and Numerical Methods

Introduction to Computer Programming and Numerical Methods

Jocelyn O. Padallan

ARCLER PRESS

www.arclerpress.com

Introduction to Computer Programming and Numerical Methods

Jocelyn O. Padallan

Arcler Press
224 Shoreacres Road
Burlington, ON L7L 2H2
Canada
www.arclerpress.com
Email: orders@arclereducation.com

ISBN: 978-1-77407-638-5 (Hardcover)

ABOUT THE AUTHOR

Jocelyn O. Padallan is Assistant Professor II from Laguna State Polytechnic University, Philippines and she is currently pursuing her Master of Science in Information Technology at Laguna State Polytechnic University San Pablo Campus and has Master of Arts in Education from the same University. She has passion for teaching and has been Instructor and Program Coordinator at Laguna State Polytechnic University

TABLE OF CONTENTS

GLOSSARY

A

Administrative – Relating to the running of a business, organization, etc.

Algorithm – An algorithm is a finite sequence of well-defined, computer-implementable instructions, typically to solve a class of problems or to perform a computation.

Alphanumeric – Consisting of or using both letters and numerals.

Antiderivative – An antiderivative, inverse derivative, primitive function, primitive integral or indefinite integral of a function f is a differentiable function F whose derivative is equal to the original function f.

Approximate Linear Programming – Approximate linear programming (LP) is a prominent method for solving factored MDPs. However, it cannot be applied to models with large treewidth due to the exponential number of constraints.

Approximation- The value or quantity that is nearly but incorrect.

Arbitrary Constant – A symbol to which various values may be assigned but which remains unaffected by the changes in the values of the variables of the equation.

Attained – Succeed in achieving (something that one has worked for).

B

Block Allocation – In computer file systems, a block allocation is a data structure used to track disk blocks that are considered "in use." Blocks may also be referred to as allocation units or clusters.

C

CNC – Is the automated control of machining tools and 3D printers by means of a computer.

Coefficients – A coefficient is a multiplicative factor in some term of a polynomial, a series, or any expression.

Conjugate – Give the different forms of (a verb in an inflected language such as Latin) as they vary according to voice, mood, tense, number, and person.

Convergence – The process or state of converging.

Coolant – Is a substance, typically liquid or gas, that is used to reduce or regulate the temperature of a system.

Curtailed – Reduce in extent or quantity; impose a restriction on.

D

Derivative – Is a way to show rate of change: that is, the amount by which a function is changing at one given point

Differential Equation – Is an equation that relates one or more functions and their derivatives.

Direct Neural Dynamic Programming – The direct neural dynamic programming (DNDP) is to be used to control a helicopter to perform realistic maneuvers and it demonstrates how this method provides an approximate solution to this optimal control problem that is often solved by dynamic programming.

Dynamic Programming – It is a method for solving a complex problem by breaking it down into a collection of simpler subproblems, solving each of those subproblems just once, and storing their solutions using a memory-based data structure (array, map, etc.).

E

Eigenvalues – Eigenvalues are a special set of scalars associated with a linear system of equations (i.e., a matrix equation) that are sometimes also known as characteristic roots, characteristic values.

Eigenvectors – Eigenvectors are a special set of vectors associated with a linear system of equations (i.e., a matrix equation) that are sometimes also known as characteristic vectors, proper vectors, or latent vectors.

Electromagnetic Device – Are devices that contain electromagnets. Examples of electromagnetic devices include doorbells and any devices that have electric motors, such as electric fans.

Electronic Fuel Injection – Electronic Fuel Injection system fitted to most modern vehicles combines sophisticated computer controls with a high-pressure fuel delivery system to provide optimum power and fuel efficiency.

Ellipse – An ellipse is a plane curve surrounding two focal points, such that for all points on the curve, the sum of the two distances to the focal points is a constant.

Elusive – Difficult to find, catch, or achieve.

Encoded – Convert into a coded form.

Exception Handling – Exception handling is the process of responding to the occurrence, during computation, of exceptions-anomalous or exceptional conditions requiring special processing-often disrupting the normal flow of program execution

Execution – The carrying out of a plan, order, or course of action.

Extrapolation – Extrapolation is a type of estimation, beyond the original observation range, the value of a variable on the basis of its relationship with another variable.

F

FCE – Is defined as a mechanical device that physically changes a process in response to a change in the control system setpoint.

Floating point Number – The Floating-point arithmetic is arithmetic in computing using formulaic representation of real numbers as an approximation to enable a trade-off between scale and accuracy.

H

Hamilton-Jacobian-Bellman Equation – The Hamilton-Jacobian-Bellman (HJB) equation gives a necessary and sufficient condition for optimality of a control with respect to a loss function. It is, in general, a nonlinear partial differential equation in the value function, which means its solution is the value function itself.

Human Error – The human error refers to something performed which was not planned by the actor; not expected by a collection of rules or an external observer; or which led the mission or process beyond its appropriate limits.

Hyperbola – A hyperbola is a type of smooth curve lying in a plane, defined by its geometric properties or by equations for which it is the solution set.

I

Imperative – of vital importance; crucial.

Inevitably – As is certain to happen; unavoidably.

Integration – An integral assigns numbers to functions in a way that can describe displacement, area, volume, and other concepts that arise by combining infinitesimal data.

Interpolation – The interpolation is a type of estimation, a way of generating new data points within the context of a fixed set of existing data points, in the statistical field of numerical analysis.

Intricate – Very complicated or detailed.

Intuitive – Using or based on what one feels to be true even without conscious reasoning; instinctive

iPods – A small electronic device for playing and storing digital audio and video files.

Iteration – Is the repetition of a process in order to generate a sequence of outcomes.

L

Linear Programming – Linear programming is a method to achieve the best outcome in a mathematical model whose requirements are represented by linear relationships. Linear programming is a special case of mathematical programming.

Loops – A program executes the sequence of statements many times until the stated condition becomes false.

M

Machine code – A computer program that is written in machine language instructions that can be executed directly by a computer's CPU.

Maple – Is a symbolic and numeric computing environment as well as a multi-paradigm programming language.

Markov Decision Process – A Markov decision process (MDP) is a discrete time stochastic control process. It provides a mathematical framework for modeling decision making in situations where outcomes are partly random and partly under the control of a decision maker.

Mathematica – Is a modern technical computing system spanning most areas of technical computing including neural networks, machine learning, image processing, geometry, data science, visualizations, and others.

Microprocessor – Is a computer processor that incorporates the functions of a central processing unit on a single integrated circuit, or sometimes up to eight integrated circuits.

Modeling Error – A mathematical model is constructed for a specific mechanism or computational mechanism.

MTR – My traceroute, originally named Matt's traceroute is a computer program which combines the functions of the traceroute and ping programs in one network diagnostic tool.

N

Non-Linear – Is such which does not form a straight line. It looks like a curve in a graph and has a variable slope value.

Notation – A series or system of written symbols used to represent numbers, amounts, or elements in something such as music or mathematics.

Numerical Error – The numerical error is the error in numerical computations in software engineering and mathematics.

O

Optimization – The action of making the best or most effective use of a situation or resource.

Overloading – The ability to create multiple functions of the same name with different implementations.

P

Parabola – A parabola is a plane curve which is mirror-symmetrical and is approximately U-shaped.

Prioritizes – Designate or treat (something) as being very or most important.

Proficient – Competent or skilled in doing or using something.

Prominent – situated so as to catch the attention; noticeable.

Propagation – The action to propagate and foster a concept, philosophy, and so on.

Q

Quasilinear – A type of differential equation where the coefficient of the highest order derivative does not depend on the derivative of the unknown function.

Qubit – A qubit is a quantum bit, the counterpart in quantum computing to the binary digit or bit of classical computing. Just as a bit is the basic unit of information in a classical computer, a qubit is the basic unit of information in a quantum computer.

R

Radio Waves – Are a type of electromagnetic radiation with wavelengths in the electromagnetic spectrum longer than infrared light.

Reinforcement Learning – Reinforcement learning is an area of machine learning concerned with how software agents ought to take actions in an environment in order to maximize the notion of cumulative reward. Reinforcement learning is one of three basic machine learning paradigms, alongside supervised learning and unsupervised learning.

Relay – Is an electrically operated switch which consists a set of input terminals for a single or multiple control signals, and a set of operating contact terminals.

Resource Allocation – In computing, resource allocation is necessary for any application to be run on the system. When the user opens any program, this will be counted as a process, and therefore requires the computer to allocate certain resources for it to be able to run.

Retrieved – Get or bring (something) back from somewhere.

Revolutionized – Change (something) radically or fundamentally.

S

Server – A computer or computer program which manages access to a centralized resource or service in a network.

Simulating – Imitate the appearance or character of.

Software – The programs and other operating information used by a computer.

Stipulating – Demand or specify (a requirement), typically as part of an agreement.

Subinterval – Any of several smaller intervals into which a larger one is divided.

T

Thermostat – Is a component which senses the temperature of a physical system and performs actions so that the system's temperature is maintained.

Truncated – Truncation is limiting the number of digits right of the decimal point.

Truncation Error – If approximation is used in numerical modeling a truncation error arises.

V

Value Functions – The value function is defined as the supremum of the objective function taken over the set of admissible controls. Given, a typical optimal control problem is subject to with initial state variable.

Vector Allocation – Vectors use a dynamically allocated array to store their elements. This array may need to be reallocated in order to grow in size when new elements are inserted, which implies allocating a new array and moving all elements to it.

W

Work piece – An object being worked on with a tool or machine.

LIST OF FIGURES

LIST OF TABLES

LIST OF ABBREVIATIONS

ADC	analog to the digital converter
ADP	approximate dynamic programming
AI	artificial intelligence
ALP	approximate linear programming
CAD	computer aided design
CAM	computer aided manufacturing
CD	compact disc
CD-ROM	compact disc, read-only-memory
CNC	computerized numerical control
COBOL	common business-oriented language
CPU	central processing unit
CRA	complex resource allocation
DC	direct current
DHP	dual heuristic dynamic programming
DNDP	direct neural dynamic programming
DVD	digital versatile disc
EFI	electronic fuel injection
FCE	final control element
FORTRAN	formula translation
GDHP	globalized dual heuristic dynamic programming
GPS	global positioning system
HDP	heuristic dynamic programming
HJB	Hamilton-Jacobian-Bellman
IEEE	Institute for Electronic and Electrical Engineering
ISO	International Organization for Standardization
LED	light emitting diode
LTE	local truncation error

MDPs	Markov decision processes
MIMO	multi input multi output
MTR	Matt's trace route
NDP	neural dynamic programming
ODE	ordinary differential equation
OOP	object-oriented programming
PDE	partial differential equation
PSE	problem solving environments
PV	process variable
RAM	random-access memory
RLN	reinforcement learning network
SISO	single input single output
SP	set point
USB	universal serial bus

PREFACE

The software has become a norm and necessity in the current time owing to the digital age that we live in. The software development is based on intense mathematical calculations and processes that a human brain is not capable of solving in a quick time. Thus, the software that is developed through numerous lines of codes, provide the basis for tedious calculations.

The software requires organized programming so that they can yield the desired results in constrained time limits. This makes the general work much easier and simplifies the whole process of evaluation, providing insights in no time. These computer programs are based on various numerical techniques that have been discovered and researched by various scholars and philosophers over the centuries.

This book takes the readers through the various kinds of numerical methods and programming techniques. It sheds light on several aspects of such techniques and also highlights the usage and application of each of those techniques in software programming. Thus, the readers get the gist of computer programming, updating themselves with the information and knowledge and the importance of such techniques.

The first chapter stresses on the fundamentals of computer programming so that the readers are clear about the concepts that form the utmost basics in the field. The second chapter takes the readers through the concepts of numerical methods and their significance.

Then, the third chapter explains the importance of class and object in the programming world. It also explains them the way in which the class and objects are created. Then, the fourth chapter introduces the readers to the concepts of arrays, functions, and the control systems and elaborates on their role in programs.

The fifth chapter throws light on the computations involving matrices and vectors, also taking the readers through the concepts of orbit. The readers are then told about the ways in which they can find solutions to the set of equations and explained interpolation and approximation to aid in the simplification of equations. The seventh chapter takes the readers through the ways in which the ordinary and partial differential equations can be solved. It elaborates on various kinds of methods to do so. The last chapter takes the readers through the subject of approximate dynamic programming and explains them the various aspects of it.

This book has been designed to suit the knowledge and pursuit of the researchers and scholars and to empower them with the various mathematical and computational methods, on which the modern computer programming is based, so that they are updated with the information. I hope that the readers find the book explanatory and insightful and that this book is referred by the scholars across several domains.

CHAPTER

1

FUNDAMENTALS OF COMPUTER PROGRAMMING

CONTENTS

This chapter discusses about the fundamentals of computer programming. This chapter emphasizes on the different types of programming languages. High-level languages and low-level languages are discussed in detail in this chapter. The further classification of these languages is also defined in the chapter. Software and hardware are an important aspect of computer and these are explained in this chapter. This chapter also explains the benefits and drawbacks of different programming languages and the uses of these languages. Different data types are also explained in this chapter.

1.1. INTRODUCTION

There are several different ways that individuals make use of computers. In educational institutes or schools, students make use of computers for tasks like searching for articles, writing some papers, sending emails, and taking part in online classes.

At workplaces or offices, individuals make use of computers to analyze the information or the data, make some presentations, conduct all the business transactions, communicate with customers as well as colleagues, control machines in manufacturing facilities, and there are a lot of other things that they do.

When people are at home, they make use of computers for tasks like doing shopping online, paying bills, communicating with their friends as well as family, and playing computer games. There are many other devices that are computers too such as iPods, cell phones, BlackBerries, car navigation systems.

The uses of computers are nearly limitless in the day to day lives. Computers can perform so many varieties of things. This is because computers can be programmed. This simply means that computers are not designed to perform just a single job, but it can perform any kind of job that their programs tell them to do.

A program is defined as a set of instructions that are followed by the computer in order to do a task.

For instance, Microsoft Word and Adobe Photoshop are the two commonly used programs. Microsoft Word is defined as a word processing program that allows an individual to create, edit, as well as print the documents with the computer. Adobe Photoshop is defined as an image editing program that allows you to work with graphic images, such as photos taken with your digital camera.

Programs are generally referred to as software. Software is very important to a computer. This is because the software controls everything that the computer does. All of the software that is used in order to make computers use is made by the people who are working as software developers or programmers.

A software developer or programmer is an individual that is having the training as well as the skills required to design, make, and test all the computer programs.

Computer programming is considered as exciting as well as a rewarding profession. In the present times, an individual will find programmers' work that is used in many fields such as government, entertainment, business, law enforcement, medicine, agriculture, academics, and there are several other fields.

There are various individuals who believe that computer programming is an arcane art. But the truth is that computer programming is just the other form of something that most of the individuals can already do. For example, when someone asked how to get to the local library, the individual reply with a program even though it is probably called "giving the directions."

The instructions may not work because there might be chances that an individual, who is giving the instructions, forget a turning, or do not count an alley as a street though the other individual, who receives the instructions, does.

This type of mistake is known as a "bug" by computer programmers. Knitting as well as the embroidery patterns are programs; in fact, they can often be transformed into a machine-readable form.

This is done by punching the instructions on a card or tape. A musical score is the other form of program that are having special symbols that have to be placed in two dimensions in a correct way.

In addition to it, a music program (score) can also be converted into some of the mechanical or electronic formats.

Because of this, devices like modern keyboards can play them automatically (and other devices like piano rolls provided such automation long before the invention of electronic computers).

Computer programming is the other way that an exact set of instructions can be provided in order to attain an objective.

1.2. HARDWARE AND SOFTWARE

The hardware of the computer is the physical devices that a computer is made of. On the other hand, software is the programs that run on a computer.

1.2.1. Hardware

The term hardware means all those components or the physical devices that makes a computer. A computer is not just a single device, but it is defined as a system of devices that all work simultaneously. It is just like the different types of instruments in a symphony orchestra. In a computer, every single device plays its important part.

An individual would have probably seen sales literature listing components like memory, microprocessors, video displays, disk drives, graphics cards, and many other components if he or she have ever shopped for a computer.

Unless an individual already have a lot of information about computers, or at least have a friend that know all about the computer, understanding what these various components do might be challenging for them. A typical computer system inside the following main components. These components include:

- The central processing unit (CPU);
- Main memory;
- Secondary storage devices;
- Output devices; and
- Input devices

*1.2.1.1. **The CPU***

It is said that the computer is running or executing the program when a computer is doing the tasks that a program tells it to do. The CPU or the CPU is defined as the part of a computer that actually runs the programs. The CPU is considered as the most important component in a computer. This is because the computer could not run software without it.

It has been observed that in the computers that were used in the early times, CPUs were huge These devices were made of electrical as well as mechanical components like vacuum tubes and switches. The ENIAC was built in 1945. This is considered by many to be the first programmable electronic computer of the World. This was built in order to calculate artillery ballistic tables for the U.S. Army. This machine which was primarily a large size CPU was 8 feet tall in height, 100 feet in length, and weighed 30 tons.

In the present times, CPUs are small chips that are called microprocessors. In addition to it, being much small in size as compared to the old electromechanical CPUs that were used in the computers in the previous times, microprocessors are also much more powerful.

1.2.1.2. Main Memory

Main memory is the primary work area of the computer. It is the main memory where the computer stores a program while the program is running, and also, the data, that the program is working with, is stored in it. For instance, suppose there is a word processing program to write an essay for the class. While he or she perform this, both the essays as well as the word processing program are stored in main memory. In addition to it, main memory is generally called random-access memory, or RAM. It is known by this name because the CPU is able to quickly access data that is stored at any random location in random-access memory (RAM).

Generally, RAM is a volatile type of memory. This is used just for temporary storage when a program is running. The contents that is stored in RAM are deleted when the computer is turned off. Inside the computer, random-access memory that RAM is stored in chips in the computer system.

1.2.1.3. Secondary Storage Devices

Secondary storage is defined as a kind of memory that can hold data or the information for a longer period of time, even when the power is cut off from the computer. It has to be noted that the programs are generally stored in secondary memory and these programs are loaded into main memory when required. In addition to it, the essential and crucial data, like payroll data, word processing documents, and inventory records, is saved to secondary storage.

Disk drive is the most common kind of secondary storage device. Data is stored in a disk drive by magnetically encoding it onto a circular disk. It has been observed that most of the computers have a disk drive that is attached inside their case. External disk drives are also available, This drive is connected to one of the communication ports of the computer. External disk drives can be used in order to make the backup copies of the essential and the crucial data or to move data to the other computer.

Apart from the external disk drives, there are various types of devices that have been created for the purpose of copying the data and is also used for moving the data to the other computers. It has been observed that for so many years, floppy disk drives were popular.

The data is stored by a floppy disk drive onto a small floppy disk. This data can be deleted from the drive. In addition to all the advantages of floppy disks, there are so many disadvantages. Some of these disadvantages are that these disks hold only a small amount of data, can be unreliable and they are slow to access data.

It has been observed that in the recent years, the use of floppy disk drives has dropped dramatically. The use of superior devices like USB drives increased. USB drives are defined as the small devices that plug into the universal serial bus (USB) port of the computer. These USB drives appear to the system as a disk drive. However, there is no disk involved in these drives.

The data is stored in a special kind of memory by these drives. This special kind of memory is called flash memory. USB drives are also called by several other terms such as memory sticks and flash drives. There are some advantages of these USB drives. Some of these advantages are that they are really cheap that is of low cost, reliable, and portable that is small enough to be carried in the pocket.

There are various optical devices like the compact disc (CD) and the digital versatile disc (DVD). These devices are also popular for the purpose of storing the data. On an optical disc, the data is not recorded magnetically, but the data is encoded as a series of pits on the surface of the disc.

In addition to it, CD and DVD drives make use of a laser in order to detect the pits and therefore, read the data that is encoded. A large amount of data is stored in optical discs. CD and digital versatile drives (DVD) are good mediums for making the backup copies of data. This is because recordable CD and DVD drives are now commonplace.

1.2.1.4. Input Devices

Input is defined as the data that is collected by the computer from people and from some other devices. Input device is defined as the component that collects the data from people and other devices and sends it to the computer. Some of the common input devices are the mouse, scanner, keyboard, microphone, and digital camera. In addition to it, optical devices and disk drives can also be considered as input devices. This is because programs as well as the data are retrieved from them and then it is loaded into the memory of the computer.

1.2.1.5. Output Devices

Output is defined as the data the computer produces for individuals or for some other devices. It is just the opposite of input devices. This data might be a list of names, a sales report, or a graphic image. Output devices receives the data and then formats and presents the data. Some of the common output devices are printers and video displays. In addition to it, CD recorders and disk drives can also be considered as output devices. This is because the system sends data to them so that it can be saved for the future use.

1.2.2. Software

Figure 1.1. Software is defined as a set of instructions that helps the computer to perform a task.

Source: Image by Flickr.

Software is necessary for the computers so that they can be functional. Everything that is done by the computer, from the time the power of computer is turned on and till it is switched off, is under the control of software. System software and application software are the two general types of software. It has been observed that most of the computer programs clearly fit into one of these two classifications of software (Figure 1.1).

1. **System Software:** The programs that helps in controlling and managing the fundamental operations of a computer are generally known as system software. Generally, system software consists of the following kinds of programs:

   i. Operating Systems: An operating system is considered as the most fundamental set of programs on a computer. It performs various functions. The internal operations of the computer's hardware are controlled by the operating system. In addition to it, it also manages all of the devices that are connected to the computer. It also allows data to be saved to and recovered from storage devices. Apart from all these functions, it also allows other programs to run on the computer.

ii. Utility Programs: A specialized task is performed by a utility program. This task helps in improving the operation of computer or safeguards the data. File compression programs, virus scanners, and data backup programs are the examples of utility programs.

2. **Software Development:** Software development tools are defined as the programs that are used by the programmers in order to create, modify, and test the software. Some of the examples of programs that falls in to this classification are compilers, assemblers, and interpreters.

3. **Application Software:** Application software are defined as the programs that make a computer valuable for day to day tasks. These are considered as the programs that the individuals usually spend most of their time running on the computers.

1.3. UNDERSTANDING A COMPUTER PROGRAM

A program is defined as a collection of a set of instructions or operations. These instructions or operations are organized in such a manner that they are performed or carried out in a systematic way. Let's take an example of program that is used for the calculation of the product of two matrices. In this program, the values of elements of the two matrices are given as input to the program.

The code or the steps or the statements (that is program lines) are included in the. These codes or steps are used to find the elements of the product matrix and write down the outcomes either on the screen of the computer or on any file on the computer. Let's take some other example of a complex program like the program that handles the railway reservations in some developing countries. The program runs on some "large" computer. This is known as a server.

The program has the entire data or the information on the availability of the seats on all the trains. An individual who want to book a seat or a berth logs into the system by the help of the internet (through internet he/she has already made an account on the reservation system's program), gives the information that is needed for reservation. He or she gets an output on the screen if a reservation of seat is available as required. This output is the ticket which can then be printed out. The person has to pay the amount that is required via internet banking.

Therefore, it can be concluded from the above examples that some of the elements in a program are output, input, repeated operations (like computing each element of a matrix one by one), information storage, comparisons (that is the seat is available or not), performing mathematical operations like multiplications, additions and some other functions like those functions that are found on a calculator. By the use of these features, it is feasible to design or to write 2 programs for helping highly complex functions like running unmanned trains, automatic landing on the moon or for mobile communications.

In addition to it, there are various programming languages like java, FORTRAN, and C++. It has been observed that some of the languages are not used any longer like basic or Pascal. This may give rise to new languages. But the main focus has always been on programming.

The compilers (for FORTRAN, java, and C++) that are used to convert the program code into a form or file that can be further executed on the computer (such a kind of file is known as an executable file) are available freely.

1.3.1. Algorithms

It has been observed that in the previous days of programming it was a common practice to make the flow chart for a task that is required to be carried out. It is less common these Days. The essential preparation before writing any of the program is to have the knowledge about the algorithm for resolving the problem at hand.

An algorithm is defined as a set of well-defined steps that are required to be carried out for providing a solution to a problem. One cannot solve the problem it there is any ambiguity in a step. Consider the following statements:

- If the real number x is assigned a negative actual value i.e. if $x < 0$, then the absolute value is-x, and
- Take the square root of object 'w.'

IT has been observed that the statement 'a' is unambiguous and statement b is vague in the above-mentioned statements. This is because if the object 'w' is a word then its square root cannot be taken. The square root is again the problem if the object 'w' is a negative number, until, and unless the complex number come in to play and are to dealt with.

1.3.2. Variables

One would like to think of the old result while working with the calculator. The old result is remembered so that it can be used later without typing it again. This can be done by declaring a variable:

Declare X=9999*9999

This declares X and binds it to 99980001. This variable can be used later on:

{Browse X*X}

The answer 9996000599960001 is displayed.

Variables are only considered as the short-cuts for values. This means that the variables cannot be assigned more than once. But another variable can be declared with the same name as the earlier one. It means that the previous one is no longer available. But all the calculations that were done earlier, which used the old variable, are the same that is they are not changed. The reason behind this is there are in fact two concepts that are hiding behind the word "variable":

The identifier. This is what is typed in as input.

Variables begin with a capital letter and it can be further followed by any letters or digits. For instance, the capital letter "X" can be a variable identifier.

The store variable. This is what the system uses to performs the calculation. It is part of the system's memory, which is known as the store of the system.

A new store variable is created by declare statement and it creates the variable identifier refer to it. All the previous calculations that used the same identifier X are the same. There is no change because the identifier refers to the other store variable.

1.3.3. Functions

Let's take some of the examples of more involved calculation. Assume that there is the need to perform the calculation of the factorial function n!. This is explained as $1 \times 2 \times \cdots \times (n - 1) \times n$. This provided the number of permutations of n items. This means that it provided the number of several ways these items can be put in a row. Factorial of 10 is:

{Browse 1*2*3*4*5*6*7*8*9*10}

3628800 is displayed. For examples, there is the need to calculate the factorial of 100. Now, all the tedious calculation part of typing the integer from 1 to 100 has been left to be done by the system. In order to calculate the factorial of any number n, the system will be trained by program to perform the calculation by defining a function:

Declare fun {Fact N}

if N==0 then 1 else N*{Fact N-1} end

The keyword "end" declare tells that there is the need to define something new. A new function is started by the keyword fun. The function is known as Fact and it has one argument N. The argument is defined as a local variable. This means that it is known just inside the function body. Thee=re is the declaration of a new variable each time the function is called.

1. **Recursion:** The function body is an instruction called an if expression. There are following steps that are performed by if expression when the function is called:

It first confirms whether N has to the value equal to that of 0 by performing the test N==0.

If in case the test is successful, then the expression after the then is computed. Number 1 is returned. This is because 1 is the factorial of 0.

On the other hand, if the test does not succeed, then the expression after the else is computed. This means that if N is not having the value equal to that of 0, then the expression N*{Fact N-1} is done. This expression makes use of Fact, the very function that is defined. This is known as recursion.

It is completely normal and no cause for alarm. Fact is recursive. This is because the factorial of N is simply N times the factorial of N-1. Fact make use of the following mathematical definition of factorial:

$0! = 1$

$n! = n \times (n - 1)!$ if $n > 0$. This is recursive.

Executing this function:

{Browse {Fact 10}}. 3628800 is displayed as it was displayed previously. This provides the confidence that Fact is performing the correct calculation. Let's take an example of a bigger input:

{Browse {Fact 100}}

As an outcome, a huge number will be displayed:

933 26215 44394 41526 81699 23885 62667 00490

71596 82643 81621 46859 29638 95217 59999 32299

15608 94146 39761 56518 28625 36979 20827 22375

82511 85210 91686 40000 00000 00000 00000 00000

This is a case of arbitrary precision arithmetic. It is sometimes known as "infinite precision" even though it is not infinite. The precision is restricted by how much memory does the system has. It has been observed that a typical low-cost personal computer which is having 64 MB of memory can deal with hundreds of thousands of numbers.

2. **Combinations:** There is an example of a function that is used to calculate the number of combinations of r items that are taken from n. This is equivalent to the number of subsets of size r. This can be made from a set of size n. In mathematical notation, this is written as 'nr' and it is pronounced "n choose r." It can be well-defined as follows by the use of the factorial: nr

= n!r! (n – r)!

This naturally leads to the function that is mentioned below:

```
Declarefun {Comb N R}
{Fact N} div ({Fact R}*{Fact N-R})
end
```

For instance, {Comb 10 3} is 120. This is the number of methods that 3 items can be taken from 10. This is not the most effective manner to write Comb, but this method is possibly the simplest one.

1.4. TYPES OF PROGRAMMING LANGUAGES

Basically, there are two kinds of computer programming languages that are mentioned below:

- Low level language; and
- High level language.

1.5. LOW LEVEL LANGUAGES

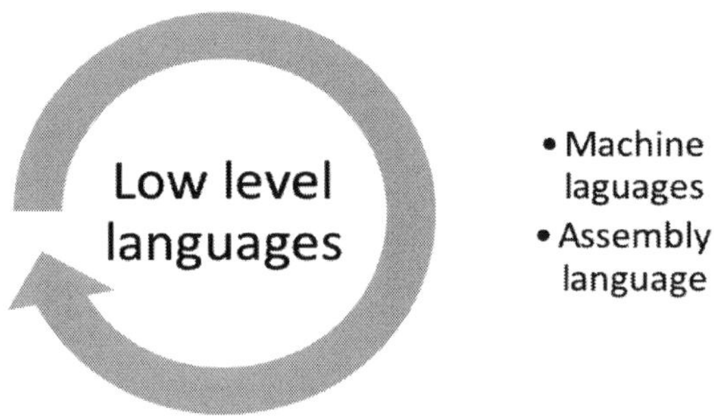

Figure 1.2. Machine language and assembly language are the low-level languages.

Low level language is defined as the programming language that is very close to machine code (0s and 1s) (Figure 1.2).

The program instructions that are written in these languages are in binary form.

Some of the examples of low-level languages are:

- Assembly language; and
- machine language.

1.5.1. Machine Language

The instructions in binary form is known as a machine language or it can also be called machine code. These instructions in binary form can be understood directly by the computer (CPU) without even translating.

Many experts call machine language as the first generation of programming language. Machine language is defined as the fundamental language of the computer. All the program instructions that are written in this language are in the binary form (this means it is in the form of 0's and 1's).

It has to be noted that for different computers, this language is different.

It is difficult to learn the machine language.

Advantage of Machine Language

- The program of machine language runs very fast. This is because there is no need of translation program for the CPU. This the single advantage of machine language.

Disadvantage of Machine Language

Some of the main disadvantages of machine languages:

- **Machine Dependent:** The internal design of every single computer is not same from every other kind of computer; machine language also varies from one computer to the other computer. Therefore, if a company, after becoming competent or proficient in the machine language of one kind of computer, decides to change to the other type, then it is the duty of the programmer to learn a new machine language. In addition to it, the programmer would have to rewrite all the existing program.
- **Difficult to Modify:** It is not easy to correct or to change this language. Examining the machine instructions in order to locate the errors is not easy and it also takes a lot time.
- **Difficult to Program:** A machine language program is executed directly as well as efficiently by the computer, but it is not that easy to program in machine language. A machine language programming must be well informed about the hardware structure of the computer.

1.5.2. Assembly Language

Assembly language is the other low-level programming language. This is because the program instructions that are written in this language are closer to the machine language.

Many of the experts also called assembly language as the second generation of programming language.

With the help of assembly language, a programmer writes the program instructions by the use of symbolic instruction code instead of using the binary codes.

Symbolic codes are important abbreviations like SUB is used for substation operation. In addition to it, MUL is used for multiply operation and so on. This, this language is also known as the low-level symbolic language.

Mnemonic code is defined as the set of program instructions that is written in assembly language. Assembly language helps in providing the facilities for controlling the hardware of the computer.

Advantage of Assembly Language

Some of the major advantages of using assembly language:

- **Easy to Understand and Use:** This language is easy to use because of the use of mnemonic code instead of using numeric op-codes and using symbolic names for data location instead of using the numeric addresses.
- **Easier to Locate and Correct Errors:** The programmers are not required to keep the track of storage location of the data as well as the instruction. There are a few errors made at the time of writing the programs in assembly language. But it is very easy to find those errors that are made and correct them.
- **Easy to Modify:** This language is easy to understand, it is very easy to find, correct, and doing some changes in the instruction of an assembly language program.
- **Efficiency of Machine Language:** It has to be noted that this assembly language program will be just as long as the resulting machine language program. Therefore, leaving out the translation time that is needed by the assembler, the actual execution time that is required for an assembly language program and its equal machine language program.

Disadvantage of Assembly Languages

Some of the main drawbacks of using assembly language are as follows:

- **Machine Dependent:** The assembly language programs are reliant on machine language. Every single instructions of assembly language program is translated into just one machine language instruction,
- **Knowledge of Hardware Required:** Assembly languages are dependent on the machine. It is must for assembly language programmer to have a good knowledge of characteristics as well as logical structure of the computer in order to write a good assembly language computer code.
- **Machine Level Coding:** Every instruction of assembly language program is replaced for just one machine language instruction. Therefore, just like machine language programs, writing the assembly language program also takes a lot of time and it is very difficult.

1.6. HIGH LEVEL LANGUAGES

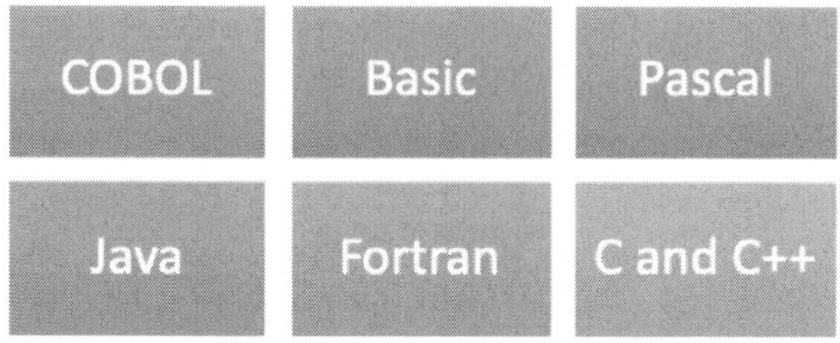

Figure 1.3. Some of the examples of high-level languages.

High level languages are the programming languages that are close to human languages (for instance, English languages) (Figure 1.3).

Some of the examples of high-level languages are as follows:

- COBOL;
- Basic;
- Pascal;
- Java;
- Fortran;
- C++; and
- C.

It has to be noted that the high-level languages are similar to that of the English language. In high level language, the program instructions are written by the use of English words, for instance, input, print, etc. But it has to be noted that each high-level language has its own rule as well as grammar for the purpose of writing program instructions. These rules are known as the syntax of the language.

The program that is written in high level language must be translated to machine code in order to run it. It has been observed that there is a translator program for each high-level language.

Further, the high-level programming languages are divided into:

- Non procedural languages;
- Procedural languages; and
- Object oriented programming languages.

Advantages of High-Level Languages

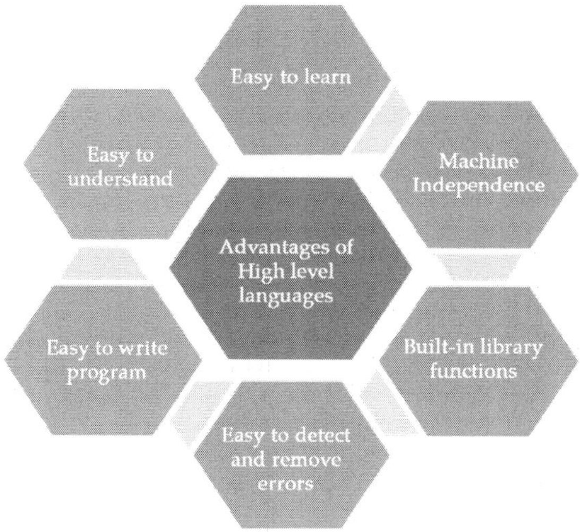

Figure 1.4. Some of the main advantages of high-level languages.

There are various benefits of high-level programming language (Figure 1.4). Some of the most important advantages of high level are as follows:

- **Easy to Learn:** These languages are easy to learn as compared to that of the low-level languages. The statements that are written for the program are same as that of the English-like statements.
- **Easy to Understand:** The program that is written in high level language by one programmer can be understood easily by the other programmer. This is because the instructions of the program are same like that of the English language.
- **Easy to Write Program:** A new program can be written very easily in a very short period of time in high level language. The larger as well as complex software can be developed in some days or in some weeks.
- **Easy to Detect and Remove Errors:** The errors that are made in a program can be detected very easily and these errors can also be removed. It has been observed that mostly the errors are occurred at the time of the compilation of new program.
- **Built-in Library Functions:** A large number of built-in functions or procedures are provided by each high-level language. These built-in functions or procedures can be used to perform particular

task at the time of designing the new programs. In such a way, a programmer saves a lot of time.

- **Machine Independence:** Program that is written in high level language is machine independent. This means that a program that is written in one kind of computer can be executed on the other type of computer.

Limitation of High-Level Language

The two most important drawbacks of high-level languages are as follows:

Efficiency: A program that is written in high level languages has lower efficiency as compared to the program that is written in a machine language or assembly language to do the similar kind of job. This means that the resultant of the program written in high level languages result is multiple machine language instruction. These instructions may not be optimized. These instructions may take more time to execute and also they need more memory space.

Less Flexibility: High level languages are less flexible as compared to that of the assembly languages. This is because they usually do not have instructions or mechanism to control the CPU, memory, and register of a computer.

1.6.1. Procedural Language

It has to be noted that procedural languages are also called third generation languages (3GLs). A program is designed by the use of procedures in a procedural language.

A procedure is defined as a sequence of instructions that is having a unique name. The instructions of the procedure are implemented with the reference of its name.

The program instructions are written in a sequence or in a specific order in procedural programming languages. In the sequence order or specific order, they must be executed in order to solve a particular problem. This means that the order (sequence order or specific order) of program instructions is essential.

Some of the popular procedural languages are mentioned and explained below:

FORTRAN: Fortran was developed in the year 1957 for IBM computers. This language stands for formula translation. It was the first high level programming language that was used to introduce the idea of modular programming. It has been observed that this language has been modified many times. The most commonly used version if this language is FORTRAN 77

COBOL: Cobol was developed in the year 1959. This language stands for common business-oriented language. This high-level language was particularly developed for business as well as commercial applications. In addition to it, this language was appropriate for managing large amount of data like:

- To process credit as well as debit account;
- To make payroll; and
- To manage the inventory system and various other business applications.

Pascal: In the honor of Blaise Pascal, this programming language is named. Blaise is a mathematician and scientist who created the first mechanical calculator. It is a structured programming language and is common in computer science development in the year 1971. This language is proper for scientific field.

ADA: This language is developed in the year 1980 and it is named in the honor of Lady Augusta ADA. Lady Augusta was the first computer programmer. For the development of ADA language, the high-level structure language which is known as Pascal was used as a model. ADA is a language that is mainly used for security purposes like for controlling military weapons such as missiles etc.

C Language: C language was developed by Dennis Ritchie and Brian Karnighan in the year 1972 at Bell Laboratories. It is one of the high-level languages. In addition to it, it can also support assembly language codes (that is low level codes). This is the reason C language is also known as middle level language. The program that is written in C can be compiled and any kind of computer can run this program.

Or it can be said that the programs written in C language are portable. C language is defined as a structured programming language. The primary feature of C language is that, it makes use of a huge number of built-in functions in order to do several tasks. Also, the user can create its own functions.

1.6.2. Non-Procedural Languages

Non procedural programming languages are also called fourth generation languages. The order of program instructions is not important in non-procedural programming languages. The primary focus or importance is given to, what is required to be done.

With the help of anon-procedural language, the user or the programmer writes English such as instructions to retrieve data from databases. These languages are simple and easy to use as compared to that of the procedural languages. In addition to it, these languages also provide the program development tools, that are user-friendly, to write instructions. The users or the programmers do not have to spend much of their time for coding the program.

The most significant non procedural languages as well as tools are mentioned and explained below:

- **SQL** This stands for structured query language. This language is specifically used to access as well as to manipulate the data of databases. It is very popular database access language. In SQL that is structured query language, the word query indicates that this language is used to make queries (or the enquiries) to do several operations on data of database. On The Other Hand, SQL can also be used in order to create tables, delete the data, add data, update data of database tables etc.
- **RPG**: This stands for report program generator. IBM introduced this language. This language was introduced to generate the reports of the business. Generally, RPG that is report program generator is used for application development on IBM midrange computers, like AS/400.

1.6.3. Object Oriented Programming Languages

The object-oriented programming concept was created in the late period of 1960s, but it has been observed that in the present times, it has become the most popular method which is used to develop software (Table 1.1).

The software is developed by the use of a set of interfacing object in object-oriented programming, An object is an element of program that includes set of modules and data structure. The modules are also known as methods and these are used in order to access the data from the object.

Object oriented approach is the modern technique that is used to design the program. It is considered as a very easy approach. In this approach, programs are designed by the use of objects. Once an object for any program is designed then it can be used again in any other program.

It has been observed that in the present times, most popular as well as commonly used object-oriented programming (OOPs) languages are java and C++.

C and C++ (it is pronounced “C plus plus”) languages are powerful. These are general-purpose languages that are developed at Bell Laboratories. In the year 1972, the C language was created. On the other hand, the C++ language was created in the year 1983.

C# is pronounced “C sharp.” Microsoft created this language around the year 2000. This language was created for the development of applications that are based on the Microsoft.NET platform (Figure 1.5).

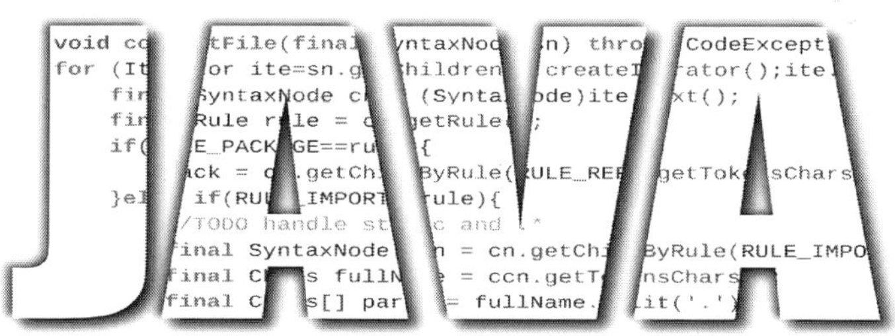

Figure 1.5. *Java is one of the high-level languages that is frequently used in present times.*

Source:ImagebyPixabay.

> Java-Sun Microsystems created Java in the early period of 1990s. This language can be used to develop programs that run on one computer or all around the Internet from a web server.

JavaScript: JavaScript was created in the period of 1990s. This language can be used in web pages. It has to be noted that JavaScript is not related to Java in spite Of its name.

Python: This language is a general-purpose language. It was created in the early period of 1990s. This language has become popular in business as well as academic applications.

Ruby: Ruby was created in the period of 1990s. It is a general-purpose language. This language is more and more becoming a popular language for all those programs that run on web servers.

Visual Basic: Visual Basic is commonly called VB. It is a Microsoft programming language and software development environment that permits all the programmers to make Windows based applications very quickly. In the early period of 1900s, Visual Basic that is VB was originally created.

Table 1.1. Difference between Procedure Oriented Programming and Object-Oriented Programming

Procedure oriented programming	Object oriented programming
The program is divided into small modules called functions.	The program is divided into number of parts called objects.
Importance is given to functions rather than data.	Emphasis is given to the data rather than procedures or functions.
It does not have any access specifier.	It has access specifiers which is names as private, public, and protected.
Most of the functions share global data.	Data is hidden and cannot be accessed by external functions.
It follows top-down approach.	It follows bottom-up approach.
It does not have any proper way for hiding data. Therefore, it is less secure.	Data hiding provides more security.
Overloading is not possible in this.	Overloading is possible in the form of function overloading and operator overloading.
FORTRAN, Pascal, C are the examples	Smalltalk, C++ are the examples

Source: Table from Airwalkbooks.com.

1.7. DATA TYPES

There is a very simple but very important concept that is available in most of the programming languages which is known as data types. As it is indicated by the name, a data type represents a kind of the data which can be processed by the use of the computer program. It can be alphanumeric, numeric, decimal, etc.

Let's take an easy example of adding two whole numbers that is 20 &30 and keeping the computer programming aside for some time. The addition of these two numbers can be simply done as follows:

20 + 30

There is another problem where two decimal numbers 20.50 &30.50 can be added. This will be written as follows:

20.50 + 30.50

Both the examples that are mentioned above are straightforward. Now, there is another example in which the information of the student is recorded in a notebook. Following information is recorded in this:

Name:

Class:

Section:

Age:

Sex:

Now, the information of one student is recoded according to the given requirement:

Name: Max Payne

Class: 7th

Section: F

Age: 12

Sex: M

The first example that was mentioned above dealt with whole numbers. And the other that is the second example added two decimal numbers. On the other hand, the third example is dealing with a mix of different data. Let's put all the examples as follows:

Student name " Max Payne" is a sequence of characters which is also known as a string.

Student class "7th" has been represented by a mix of whole number and a string of two characters. Such kind of mix is known as alphanumeric.

The sections of the student have been represented by a single character which is 'F.'

The age of the student has been represented by a whole number which is 12.

The sex of the student has been represented by a single character which is 'M.'

In this way, it is realized that in the everyday life, an individual deal with various data types like characters, strings, whole numbers (that is integers), and decimal numbers (that is floating point numbers).

In the similar way, when an individual writes a computer program in order to process various kinds of data, one is required to specify the type of the data clearly; or else the computer will not be able to understand how various operations can be done on that given data.

It has to be noted that different kinds of programming language make use of different keywords in order to identify different data types. For instance, C, and Java programming languages make use of int in order to specify integer data. On the other hand, a character data type is specified by char.

1.7.1. C and Java Data Types

It has to be noted that almost same set of data types are supported by C and Java although additional data types are supported by Java. Now, there is the example of a few common data types that are supported by both the programming languages that is C and Java (Table 1.2).

Table 1.2. Various Kinds of Data Types

Type	Keyword	Value range which can be represented by this data type
Character	char	-128 to 127 or 0 to 255
Number	Int	-32,768 to 32,767 or -2,147,483,648 to 2,147,483,647
Small Number	Short	-32,768 to 32,767
Long Number	Long	-2,147,483,648 to 2,147,483,647
Decimal Number	Float	1.2E-38 to 3.4E+38 till 6 decimal places

Source: Table by tutorialpoint.com.

These data types are known as primitive data types and one can make use of these data types in order to build more complex data types. This data types are known as user-defined data type, for instance a string will be a sequence of characters.

1.7.2. Python Data Types

There are five standard data types in Python. But this programming language that is Python does not make use of any keyword in order to highlight a specific data type. Instead this programming language is intelligent enough to understand a given data type automatically.

- String;
- Number;
- Tuple;
- List; and
- Dictionary.

Here, string represents a sequence of characters which is having a length of 1 character or more than 1 characters. On the other hand, Number specifies all types of numbers that is including decimal numbers.

1.8. VARIABLES

Variables are the names you give to computer memory locations which are used to store values in a computer program.

For example, assume you want to store two values 10 and 20 in your program and at a later stage, you want to use these two values. Let's see how you will do it. Here are the following three simple steps:

- Create variables with appropriate names;
- Store your values in those two variables; and
- Retrieve and use the stored values from the variables.

1.8.1. Creating Variables

In computer programming, the process of creating variables is also called declaring variables. There are several computer languages that are being used in the world. These different programming languages have varied methods of declaring variables inside a program. Here, the process of declaring a variable is explained with the help of an example of a program of C programming language. Amongst all the computer languages, C programming has the following simple way of creating variables:

```
#include <stdio.h>
int main ()
{
int a;
int b;
}
```

The above given program is a sample program that explains how the variables are created or declared. In this example, two variables are created in order to reserve two memory locations with the names ‘a’ and ‘b.’

These variables have been declared with the use of ‘int’ keyword. The ‘int’ keyword is used to mention the data type of the variable. Mentioning the data type indicates the type of value that will be stored with the help of variable. In this example, the values that are stored are the integer values.

In the similar manner, variables can be declared for storing values of different data types such as long, float, char or any other data type. For example:

```
/* variable to store long value */
long x;
/* variable to store float value */
float y;
```

There is another method for declaring various variables of similar type. This can be done by creating or declaring all the variables of same data type by putting them in a single line and separating them by commas as follows:

```
#include <stdio.h>
int main ()
{
int a, b;
}
```

Some of the major points about the variables, that every individual must keep in mind, are as:

- The name of a variable name can only store or possess a single type of value. For instance, if variable ‘a’ has been defined by the ‘int’ data type, then it can only store an integer value.
- Different programming languages follow different paths for variable declaration. For instance, in C programming language, there is a need for variable creation for the variable. Value creation refers to the process of declaring the variable before using it in the program. In C programming, a variable cannot be used in the program if it is not created or declared. On the other hand, programming language such as Python permits the usage of a variable name without creating or declaring it.

- Any variable that has already been declared in the program cannot be used again. A variable name can be used only once inside any program. For instance, a variable 'x' has been declared to store an integer value. Then, the variable 'x' cannot be used or declared again to define or store any other value of other data type.
- Some of the programming languages, such as Python, PHP, Perl, etc., allow declaration of data type at the time of usage of the value. These programming languages does not require declaration or specifying the data type at the time of creating variables. So, it is possible to store integer, float, or long without declaring or specifying the data type of the value.
- Any name can be given to a variable such as age, sex, salary, year 1990. Giving a name to the value is totally up to the discretion of the user. But almost every programming language permits only the usage of limited characters in their variables names. In the beginning phase of the programming, the users are suggested to use only characters in between a....z, A....Z, 0....9 as the characters for naming their variables.
- Almost every programming language requires the name of the variable to start with alphabet and not a digit. So, while naming a variable, the user must not keep the first character as a number. For example, '1990 year' will be an invalid variable name. On the other hand, year 1990 or year 1990 are valid variable names that can be used in the programs.
- Every programming language usually provides specific rules that related to creating or declaring variables in their programs. The users can learn about the rules for a particular programming language as they study about that programming language in detail.

1.8.2. Store Values in Variables

After creating or declaring the variables, it is necessary to learn how to store the values in those variables. The process of storing the value in the variable can be understood buy this example.

```
#include <stdio.h>
int main ()
{
```

```
int f;
int g;
f = 10;
g = 20;
}
```

In the above program, two additional statements are added. In these statements, the values 10 and 20 are being stored in the variables f and g respectively. It has been observed that almost every programming language has similar method of storing values in variable.

The method of storing a value to a variable can be easily identified in the program of any programming language. In any program, the variable name is always kept at the left-hand side of an equal sign '=' and the value, that the user wants to store in the variable, is always kept value on the right-hand side of the equal side.

Now, these are the major two steps. First major step is the creation of the two variables. Second step is storing the needed values in the variables that have been declared in the first step.

Completing these two steps means that the variable 'f' has the value 10 and variable 'g' has the value 20. In other words, it can be inferred that when the above program is executed, the memory location named 'f' will possess the value 10 and the memory location 'g' will possess the value 20.

1.9. ACCESS STORED VALUES IN VARIABLES

If the stored values in the variables are not to be used in the program, then there is no significance of creating or declaring the variables and storing the values in them.

After allocating the values to the variables or storing the values in them, the values must be used for any purpose. The above program consists of two variables 'f' and 'g' and they store the values 10 and 20, respectively. One of the most basic functions that can be executed with the help of above program is printing the values that has been stored to these variables.

The values assigned to these variables can be printed by the program written below:

```
#include <stdio.h>
int main ()
```

```
{
int f;
int g;
f = 10;
g = 20;
print f (“Value of f = %d\n,” f);
print f (“Value of g = %d\n,” g);
}
```

When the above program is executed, the results, that are attained, are:

Value of f = 10

Value of g = 20

In the above program, it is evident that print f () function has been used to print the statements or the values stored in the variables.

It has been observed that the function ‘%d’ is used for printing the values. This function can be replaced with the values of the given variable in print f () statements.

In the program written below, it is shown that it is possible to print both the values using a single print f () statement.

```
#include <stdio.h>
int main ()
{
int f;
int g;
f = 10;
g = 20;
print f (“Value of f = %d and value of g = %d\n,” f, g);
}
```

When the above program is executed, it produces the following result:

Value of f = 10 and value of g = 20

If the user wants to use the ‘float’ data type for their variable in C programming, then they might have to use %f instead of %d. Also, if the user wants to print a character value, then they must have to use %c. In the similar manner, various data types can be printed with the help of using ‘%’ and characters that are relevant to the data types.

1.9.1. Variables in Java

Below mentioned is the equivalent program written in Java programming language. This program will create two variables j and k. In the similar manner to the programs written in C programming, it will assign 10 and 20 in these variables. Finally, the values assigned to the variables will be printed in two ways:

```
public class Demo Java
{
public static void main(String []args)
{
int j;
int k;
j = 10;
k = 20;
System.out.println("Value of j =" + j);
System.out.println("Value of k =" + k);
System.out.println("Value of j =" + j + " and value of k =" + k);
}
}
```

After executing the above written program, the result attain will be as follows:

```
Value of j = 10
Value of k = 20
Value of j = 10 and value of k = 20
```

1.9.2. Variables in Python

In Python programming language, the program is written in a different way. The program, analogous to the programs written in the other programming languages, is written in Python. This program will help in creating two variables m and n and at the same time, assign 10 and 20 in those variables.

Python does not want the user to declare or create the data type at the time of variable creation. In fact, Programs written in Python do not need to create or declare variables in advance.

```
m = 10
n = 20
print "Value of m =," m
print "Value of n =," n
print "Value of m =," m, " and value of n =," n
```

When the above program is executed, it produces the following result:

```
Value of m = 10
Value of n = 20
Value of m = 10 and value of n = 20
```

In similar manner, the user can use the following syntax in C and Java programming to declare variables and assign values at the same time:

```
#include <stdio.h>
int main ()
{
int p = 10;
int q = 20;
printf("Value of p = %d and value of q = %d\n," p, q);
}
```

After the above written program are executed, the following result are attained:

```
Value of p = 10 and value of q = 20
```

1.10. CONCLUSION

There are various important aspects of computer programming. The application of computer programming in various tasks such as numerical calculations requires the programmer to have the highest knowledge of the basics of computer programming. In the modern world, there are various OOP languages such as C++, Java, and Python. All have the same concepts but have some variations in the methods and syntax of creating a program. Thus, in order to gain command over any of these majorly used languages, any programmer must have a thorough knowledge of the fundamental of computer programming.

REFERENCES

1. (n.d). Chapter-2: Elements of Computer Programing-1. [ebook] Available at: https://ether.chem.iitb.ac.in/~bltembe/pdfs/Comp_Chem_Chapter_2.pdf (accessed on 4 June 2020).
2. Codescracker.com. (2019). Types of Computer Programming Languages. [online] Available at: https://codescracker.com/computer-fundamental/types-of-computer-languages.htm (accessed on 4 June 2020).
3. Glassborow, F., & Allen, R., (2004). A Beginner's Introduction to Computer Programming. [ebook] West Sussex: John Wiley & Sons Ltd. Availableat:https://doc.lagout.org/Others/Francis%20Glassborow%20%26%20Roberta%20Allen%20-%20A%20Beginner%27s%20Introduction%20to%20Computer%20Programming.pdf (accessed on 4 June 2020).
4. Mathivanan, D., Rajalakshmi, D., Sathiyavathi, R., Anu, D., & Narayanan, L., (2017). Computer Programming and Numerical Methods. [ebook] Chennai: AIRWALK PUBLICATIONS. Available at: http://airwalkbooks.com/images/pdf/pdf_31_1.pdf (accessed on 4 June 2020).
5. Pearsonhighered.com. (2020). Introduction to Computers 1 and Programming. [online] Available at: https://www.pearsonhighered.com/assets/samplechapter/0/3/2/1/0321537114.pdf (accessed on 4 June 2020).
6. Roy, P., & Haridi, S., (2003). Concepts, Techniques, and Models of Computer Programming. [ebook] Swedish Institute of Computer Science. Available at: http://citeseerx.ist.psu.edu/viewdoc/download?doi=10.1.1.102.7366&rep=rep1&type=pdf (accessed on 4 June 2020).
7. Tutorialspoint.com. (2020). Computer Programming-Data Types-Tutorialspoint. [online] Available at: https://www.tutorialspoint.com/computer_programming/computer_programming_data_types.htm (accessed on 4 June 2020).
8. Usman, O., Ogunsanwo, G., Owoade, A., Abimbola, B., & Lateef, U., (2016). Introduction to Computer Programming (BASIC). [ebook] Ogun State: Tai Solarin University of Education. Available at: https://www.researchgate.net/publication/317182495_INTRODUCTION_TO_COMPUTER_PROGRAMMING_BASIC (accessed on 4 June 2020).

CHAPTER

2

AN OVERVIEW TO NUMERICAL METHODS

CONTENTS

In the chapter, an overview to numerical methods, general introduction and historical background of numerical methods is discussed.

The chapter also discuss the actual meaning and types of numerical methods. The chapter also highlighted the properties of numerical methods. In addition, the significance of numerical methods is also demonstrated in this chapter. The chapter also tries to explain why there is need to study numerical methods. Moreover, some of the errors in the possible errors that can be occurred in numerical methods is also explained.

The chapter also explain the numerical analysis and an early mathematical model in numerical methods. The chapter also throw some light on modern application and computer software in numerical methods. In the end, the chapter tries to explain numerical methods with some powerful computer tools.

2.1. INTRODUCTION

Numerical analysis refers to the study of algorithms that make use of numerical approximation (in contrast to symbolic manipulations) for solving the problems of mathematical analysis (that can be easily differentiate from discrete mathematics). It is generally seen that numerical analysis can easily finds application in almost all the arenas of the physical sciences and engineering. But it was discovered that in the 21st century, also the social sciences, life sciences, business, medicine, and even the arts have implemented essentials of scientific computations.

Within the past few years, the significant growth observed in the computing power has revolutionized the use of realistic mathematical models in both engineering and science department, and there is need of elusive numerical analysis for implementation of the comprehensive models of the world.

For instance, ordinary differential equations (ODEs) which are in existence of celestial mechanics (anticipating the motions of stars, planets, and galaxies); numerical linear algebra is very crucial for data analysis; Markov chains and stochastic differential equations are essential in simulating living cells in the field of biology and medicine.

Before the introduction of modern computers, numerical methods which were primarily relied upon on hand interpolation formulas often applied to data from large printed tables. Since the middle of 20th century, computers took this task of calculation of required functions, but majority of these formulas nonetheless consistently used as an important element of algorithms.

It can be right to assume that numerical point of view can be dated back to as early as when mathematical writings were started. A tablet designed by the Yale Babylonian Collection (YBC 7289), play critical role in giving a numerical approximation of the square root of 2, the length of the diagonal in a unit square.

It is worth noticing that numerical analysis will continue to be part of this long tradition: instead of exact symbolic answers that can be only applicable to real-world measurements by conversion into digits, it provides approximate solutions with error of certain standard.

The primary objective of the field of numerical analysis is the analysis and design of techniques in order to get the approximation but accurate exact solutions to complicated problems, the range of which is demonstrated as follows:

- It is important to note that the advanced numerical methods are very crucial in ensuring feasible anticipation of numerical weather.
- For computation of trajectory of a spacecraft, there is need of precise numerical solution of a system having ODEs.
- Car manufacturers that want to improve their standard of crash safety need to make use of computer simulations in order to avoid car crashed to a greater extent. These kinds of simulations often requires to numerically solve partial differential equations (PDEs).
- Hedge funds (which are known as private investment funds) make use of these tools from every fields of numerical analysis in a way to compute the values of stocks and derivatives with more preciseness and accuracy in comparison to other market participants.
- Airlines make use of these sophisticated optimization algorithms in order to get an estimation of ticket prices, crew assignments, airplane, and fuel needs. Historically, these kinds of algorithms were developed within the overlapping field of operations research.
- Insurance companies make use numerical programs for their actuarial analysis tasks.

2.1.1. History

The numerical analysis field necessitate the invention of advance computers by many centuries. Linear interpolation has been in use for more 2000 years. Some of the great mathematicians of the past were using numerical analysis for a prolonged period of time, as is obvious from the names of imperative algorithms such as Lagrange interpolation polynomial, Newton's method, Gaussian elimination, or Euler's method.

In order to make the computations process possible by hand, there were production of large books having ample formulas and tables of data such as function coefficients and interpolation points. With the help of these tables, usually calculated out to 16 decimal places or more for some functions, one can take an estimation of values in order to plug it into the formulas given and get the accurate numerical estimates of some functions.

It was observed that a mechanical calculator, was also developed as a tool for hand computation. These calculators were integrated into the electronic computers in the year 1940s, and then later on, it was found that these computers play very important role for administrative purposes.

But the establishment of this computer also induced the field of numerical analysis, since now it is possible to do more longer and complicated calculations in a limited period of time.

2.1.2. Direct and Iterative Methods

Direct methods refer to methods that help in computation of solution for a problem in a limited number of steps. These methods would help in giving the accurate answer if they were executed in infinite precision arithmetic.

Some example of this include the QR factorization, and Gaussian elimination method for solving the simple method of linear programming, and systems of linear equations. In practice, finite precision is mostly used the result is a calculation of the true solution (assuming consistency).

As opposite to direct methods, iterative methods cannot be projected to dismiss in a limited number of steps. Beginning from a preliminary guess, iterative methods form successive approximations that help in ensuring the exact solution but with limited application.

A convergence test, that usually entails the residual, is stated in order to determine when an adequate precise solution has (hopefully) been found. Even with the help of infinite precision arithmetic, it is not possible for these methods to reach the solution within a limited number of steps (in general).

Some example of this include the bisection method, Newton's method, and Jacobi iteration. In computational matrix algebra, these iterative methods are much needed for more complicated problems.

These methods are more common as compared to direct methods in numerical analysis. Some of these methods are direct in principle but are majorly used as though they were not, e.g., the conjugate gradient and GMRES method.

For such kind of methods, the total steps required for getting the exact solution is so large that an approximation can be accepted in the similar manner as for an iterative method.

2.1.3. Discretization

In addition, the problems which are consistent in nature can be sometime replaced by a discrete problem whose solution is renowned to approximate that of the consistent problem; such process is known by the name 'discretization.' For instance, the solution of a differential equation is a function. This function can be represented by a limited quantity of data, for example, by its value at a limited number of points at its domain, although this domain is a continuum.

2.2. MEANING OF NUMERICAL METHODS

Numerical methods can be defined as methods primarily designed for the constructive solution of mathematical problems demanding specific numerical results, majorly on a computer. A numerical method is often an unambiguous and a complete set of procedures for finding solution to a problem, accompanied with computable error estimates. Having a comprehensive understanding and implementation of such methods is the province of numerical analysis.

2.3. PROPERTIES OF NUMERICAL METHODS

It is important to note that the following criteria are critical for the performance of a numerical algorithm:

1. **Consistency:** The discretization of a PDE should become exact as the mesh size tends to zero (truncation error should vanish). It means that the result it gives should be consistent in nature. It should not be varying from one another, which are more prone to errors.

2. **Stability:** Numerical errors which are produced at the time of finding solution of discretized equations should not be magnified. It should be of stable in nature in order to get the accurate results.
3. **Convergence:** It is important to note that the numerical solution should approach the precise solution of the PDE and converge to it as the mesh size seems to zero.
4. **Conservation:** Underlying conservation laws should be appreciated at the discrete level (in addition, it is also important to avoid mock sinks/ sources).
5. **Boundedness:** Quantities such as temperatures, densities, concentrations etc. should be free from false or fake wiggles and remain nonnegative.

2.4. SIGNIFICANCE OF NUMERICAL METHODS

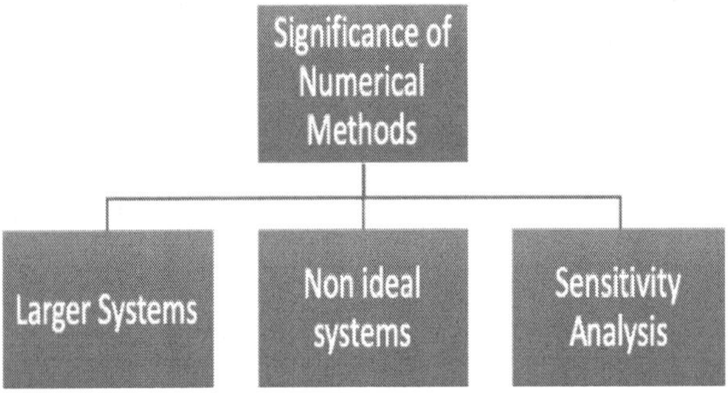

Figure 2.1. Significance of numerical methods.

Numerical methods refer to the various techniques and strategies by which mathematical problems are formed and designed, so that they can be elucidated with the help of arithmetic operations. While numerical methods can be categorized into many kinds, majority of them have one thing in common: a large number of lengthy arithmetic calculations (Figure 2.1).

Apart from numerical methods, there other two imperative methods of problem solving are graphical methods and analytical methods. The former one is not that useful as it is not accurate because its graphs are designed physically by hands.

This resulted in making the process complicated lengthy. Another constraint is its practicability for problems carrying three or less than three dimensions. It is worth noticing that the use of analytical methods can help in gaining an insight into the behavior and characteristics of a particular system.

Unfortunately, they are only applicable at systems that can be estimated through use of linear models. Since practical problems consist of both nonlinear and complex processes, it is not adequate at all to just use analytical methods.

Traditionally, both graphical and analytical methods were preferred because of time consuming characteristics of numerical methods explained above. It is often seen that various arithmetic operations consumed huge time as the only existing tools in hand were calculators, slide rules, pencil, and paper. The higher the number of operations performed, the higher the chance of a wrong outcome because of a human blunder.

At present time, with the economic and easily accessibility of computers, there has been significant change in the perception about numerical methods and reformed the ways how problem is solved. It is important to note that a computer can perform millions of calculations in just a second. Thus the speed bottleneck concerned with numerical methods has been removed.

In the field of engineering, numerical methods play very important role as they make it possible to get comprehensive understanding about the various systems in the numerous streams of engineering. It is possible only because of the fact that it prioritizes the right stages of problem solving. There are basically three stages of problem solving in engineering practice:

- Formulation;
- Solution; and
- Interpretation.

While analytical methods have their major focus on the solution stage (in a way to get a simplified model to output an answer), the various strategies and techniques used in numerical methods emphasize on the interpretation and formulation stages. The formulation stage is concerned with finding the best relationship between the dimensions of the problem and the fundamental laws of nature. Since computing power has revolutionized the solution stage into a time effective stage, rank is placed on formulation stage in a way to get the best possible answer.

It is also seen that numerical methods open various possibilities in the interpretation stage. Because of its easy calculations, the mathematical model setup in the formulation stage can be easily recurrently tweaked in order to gain an understanding of more about the properties of the system in question. Types of such 'tweaks':

2.4.1. Larger Systems

More components/dimensions added into the mathematical model. This resulted in making the system more realistic.

2.4.2. Non-Ideal Systems

Usually systems are solved for ideal conditions. The model can be formulated again to involve non idealized realities exists in a practical problem.

2.4.3. Sensitivity Analysis

Ensuring the integration of computational numerical methods make it possible for people to test the system for diverse inputs in a way to determine the sensitivity of the system.

Some of the activity that can be solved using numerical methods are discussed as follows:

- Solving linear equations;
- Finding roots;
- Calculus; and
- Numerical Interpolation.

Numerical methods are used in nearly every stream of engineering:

- Temperature distribution;
- Kinematics; and
- Circuitry.

2.5. WHY TO STUDY NUMERICAL METHODS?

1. **Historical Context:** In early age of about 3000 BC, computing was introduced with an instrument called ABACUS by Chinese society, that was only functioned and performed for arithmetic operation.-Slide rule by John Napier to compute a logarithmic problem as early as in the $16^{\text{th century}}$.

- An accounting machine that was invented by Blaise Pascal is refereed by the name Pascal Calculator.
- Introduction of data storage facility with the help of a punched card. By Loom Jacquard in $18^{\text{th century}}$.
- 18th Century: Charles Babbage rewarded for the innovative invention of Analytical Engine and Difference Engine.

- Later on till the date, all modern/most current computers are relied heavily on that principle.

2. **Present Context:** In a present-day scenario, computers are considered as a pronounced tool in computation of numerical problems, which plays very critical role in solving real-life mathematical, engineering, and physical problems.

However, it is generally seen that without any proper understanding of engineering problems, they will be completely useless.

2.5.1. How Is the Engineering System Understood?

- By experiment and observation; and
- Theoretical generalization and analysis.

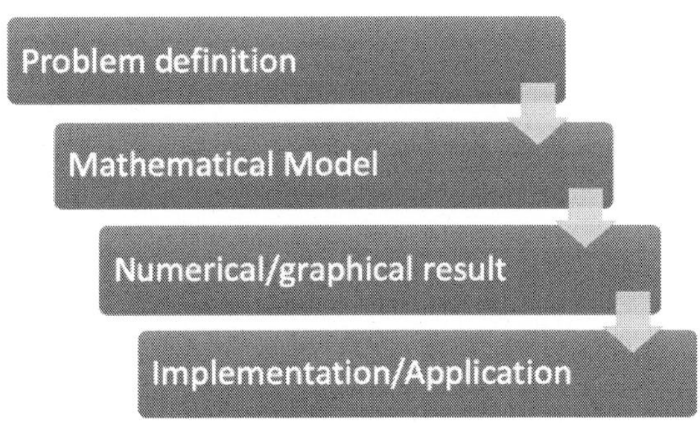

Figure 2.2. Computing process.

Source: Figure by ResearchGate

2.5.2. Analysis

It characterizes the typical mathematical model of the physical world as:

- Natural system or process in mathematical term;
- Simplification and Idealization of reality; and
- Yields productive and effective results.

2.5.3. Solution

As the mathematical model has been significantly manipulated throughout a longer period of time, it resulted in giving rise to a variety of solution for a given problem.

Analytical Vs. Numerical Solution: As it worth noticing that analytical solution is like a 'Math: a great example,' which all of us are learning all the way. Numerical solution can be computed through computer with certain approximation but getting exact result. For instance, the quadratic equation ax2+bx+c = 0 has:

- **Analytic Solution:** $x = \frac{-b \pm \sqrt{b^2 - 4ac}}{2a}$ that works for any set of given values of a, b & c. The real solution is applicable only if, i.e. the solution properties are of transparent in nature.
- **Numerical Solution:** This work only for a set of given values (a, b, c) at a certain time. In this, solution is often approximate. So, there is need for accessing estimation of error.

For this, there is need on part of computer to do repeated search until any solution is attained, but not blindly. It further demands design of a clear set of rules (steps), which is dependent on the sound mathematical reasoning and that guarantee a desired solution with adequate level of accuracy.

2.5.4. Validation and Implementation

Now, numerical method basically refers to a tool that deals with the mathematical model (articulated to describe the theory) in order to give a valid graphical or numerical result.

This example is just an archetype; as most of the actual problems (99.9%) are of complex in nature but can be solved approximately with numerical computation.

2.5.5. Summary

- It is generally seen that study of science and engineering convert physical phenomena into mathematical model often with calculation and complex-analysis.
- Numerical analysis refers to the study of procedure for finding solution to a problem with the help of a computer.
- It basically refers to the study of algorithms and further complex problems of mathematics.
- It is important to note that numerical analysis is always numerical in nature.

- The objective of numerical analysis is concerned with the analysis and design of techniques in order to give estimated but exact solution to difficult problems.

2.5.6. Applications

- It helps in forecasting of numerical weather.
- It allows to Compute trajectory of space-craft (path-of-projectile).
- It plays very important role in design and function of super computers.
- Its role in paramount in ensuring safety standard in car, resulting in avoiding of car accidents to a greater extent.

2.6. ERROR IN NUMERICAL METHODS

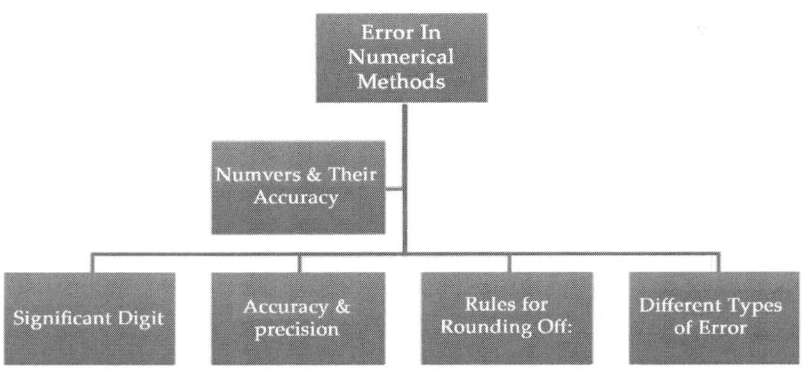

Figure 2.3. Errors in numerical methods.

2.6.1. Numbers and Their Accuracy

There are basically two categories of numbers:

- Exact numbers, for instance, 1, 2, 3 …1/2, 5/2, etc.
- Approximate numbers, for instance. PI, K …, etc.

2.6.2. Significant Digit

Digits which are primarily used to express a number referred as figures/ significant digits. The statements which help in describing the notion of significant digits are discussed as follows.

- All digits which are non-zero whether it is positive of negative.
- All zeroes arising between non-zero digits.
- Trailing zeroes succeeding a decimal point, for instance; 65.0, 3.50, 0.230 have three important digits.
- Zeroes between the decimal point are preceding a non-zero digits are not imperative, e.g., 0.001234, 0.01234, 0.0001234 all have four essential digits.
- When there is no decimal point in a digit, then trailing zeroes are not considered important, e.g., 4500 comprise only two important digits.

2.6.3. Accuracy and Precision

It is important to note that the concept of accuracy and precision are very closely associated with significant digits.

Accuracy is basically conceived as the number of important digits in a value. E.g., the number 57.345 is precise to five imperative digits.

Precision generally refers to the number of decimal positions, for instance, the range of magnitude of last digit in a value; e.g., 57.396 have a precision of 0.001.

In computation of numerical value, it is important to take into consideration numbers which have large numbers of digits and it is essential to lessen them to usable numbers of figures. This process is majorly known by the concept of rounding off. The error arises because of cut-off a large number into a usable number is referred as round-off error.

2.6.4. Rules for Rounding Off

In order to round off a number to a particular number of digits, abandon all digits located at the right of the nth digit if this discarded number is:

- Make sure that less than half a unit located in the nth place, and leave the nth digit unchanged.
- Greater than half a unit in nth place, increase the nth digit by unity.
- Exactly half a unit in the nth place, increase the nth digit by unity if it is odd; otherwise leave it unchanged.

Examples: Following numbers are rounded off to four significant figures:

1.6583 (1.658), 30.0567 (30.06), 0.859378 (0.8594), 3.14159 (3.142)

2.6.5. Different Types of Error

a) **Absolute Error:** Numerical difference between true value of a quantity and its approximate value.

Mathematically;

Absolute error (EA) = True value X – Approximate value (X1) = ΔX

b) **Relative error:** Ratio of absolute error to a true value of that quantity being concerned.

Mathematically;

$$\text{Relative Error ER} = \frac{Absolute\ Error\ (EA)}{True\ Value(X)}$$

c) **Percentage Error:** The percentage value of relative error.

Mathematically;

$$\text{Percentage Error EP} = \frac{Absolute\ Error(EA)}{True\ Valye(X)} * 100\%$$

d) **Truncation Error:** Its main reason of occurrence is because of terminating or truncation an infinite sequence of operation after a function or operation of finite number.

Example: Cos (x) = 1- x2/2,

Where ex = 1+X+X2/2

e) **Relative Accuracy:** It basically refers to the change in ratio of true value to the modulus of true value.

$$\text{Relative Accuracy (RA)} = \frac{Absolute\ Error\ (EA)}{|True\ Value(X)|} \sim \frac{Absolute\ Error\ (EA)}{|Approximate\ Value(X1)|}$$

2.7. NUMERICAL ANALYSIS

Numerical analysis is generally defined as an area of mathematics and computer science which build, interpret, and execute algorithms for numerical solution of the problems of continuous mathematics. These kinds of problems usually initiated from real-world applications of algebra, calculus, and geometry, and they entail variables that varies to a greater extent; these problems are consistent in nature and occur throughout the social sciences, natural sciences, engineering, business, and medicine sector.

During the middle of half-century, the significant growth in advance computer production and its accessibility to large number of people resulted in increasing use of realistic mathematical models in engineering and science department, and numerical analysis of growing complicated problems necessitate the need to solve these more detailed mathematical models of the world.It is generally seen that the formal academic area of numerical analysis differs from quite theoretical mathematical studies to computer science issues. With the significant increase in demand of modern-day computer for carrying out the numerical procedures in finding solution to mathematical models of the world, an area widely recognized as computational science or scientific computing and initiated during the 1980s and 1990s.

This area is majorly interested in taking a look at numerical analysis from the perspective of computer science. It is primarily concerned with using the most advanced and powerful tools of computer graphics, numerical analysis, graphical user interfaces, and symbolic mathematical computations for making it easily for their user to set up, understand, and solve complex mathematical models of the real-world situation.

2.7.1. Historical Background

It is worth noticing that the numerical algorithms are almost as old as human civilization. The Rhind Papyrus (˜1650 BC) of ancient Egypt throw light on a root finding method that help in solving a simple equation.

> Archimedes of Syracuse (287–212 BC) is responsible for creation of a new mathematics, includes the "method of exhaustion" for computation of lengths, areas, and volumes of geometric figures

When this is used as a method for finding approximations, it carries higher importance in modern numerical integration; and was considered as an important executor in the development of the calculus by Gottfried Leibnitz and Isaac Newton.

A much-needed fuel for the development of numerical procedures was the invention of the calculus by Leibnitz and Newton, as this resulted in precise mathematical models for physical reality, initially in the physical sciences and eventually in the other sciences, medicine, engineering, and business.

It is worth noticing that these mathematical models cannot be explicitly solved, and there is need of numerical methods for attaining the approximate solutions. Another critical aspect of the development of numerical methods was the formation of logarithms by Napier (1614) and others, providing a simpler way to carry out the arithmetic operations of division, multiplication, and exponentiation.

Newton was accredited with a number of numerical methods which play very crucial role in solving a variety of problems, and now he has been recognized as creator of his original ideas. One of the most important work done by him is polynomial interpolation, and root finding.

After influenced by the success of Newton, there are many other mathematics giants that came up in the 18th and 19th centuries, playing significant role in contributing to the numerical solution of mathematical problems.

Some prominent ones among them are Joseph-Louis Lagrange (1736–1813), Leonhard Euler (1707–1783), and Karl Friedrich Gauss (1777–1855). Up to the late 1800's, it seems like that majority of the mathematicians were quite broad in their interests, and many of them showed great enthusiasm and contributed heavily in numerical analysis.

2.7.2. An Early Mathematical Model

It is worth noticing that one of the most crucial and dominant mathematical models in science was that given by Newton in order to try to understand the effect of gravity. According to this model, the force of gravity on a body of mass m due to the Earth has magnitude

F = Gmme/r2

where me refers to the mass on Earth, r refers to the length of space between the canters of the two bodies, and G refers to the universal gravitational force, which is constant in nature. It is generally seen that the force on m is attributed towards the pivot of gravity of the Earth.

The gravitation model given by Newton has resulted in creation of many problems which demands solution by approximate means, often including the numerical solution of common differential equations. After the progress of basic laws of physics by Newton, it was observed that these can be applied to many physicists and mathematicians in order to give mathematical models for fluid and solid mechanics.

It came under notice that Civil and Mechanical Engineering make use of these models as the core for most modern work on the motion of fluids, solid structures. In addition to this, numerical analysis become a prerequisite for researchers in these areas of engineering.

For instance, formation of modern structures makes significant use of finite element methods in order to attain solution for the PDEs connected with models of stress; and computational fluid mechanics is now considered a foundation tool for designing of new airplanes.

In the 19th century, phenomena involving electricity, heat, and magnetism were modeled successfully; and in the 20th century, quantum mechanics, relativistic mechanics, and other theoretical constructs were created to lengthen and enhance the applicability of earlier ideas.

2.8. AN OVERVIEW OF NUMERICAL ANALYSIS

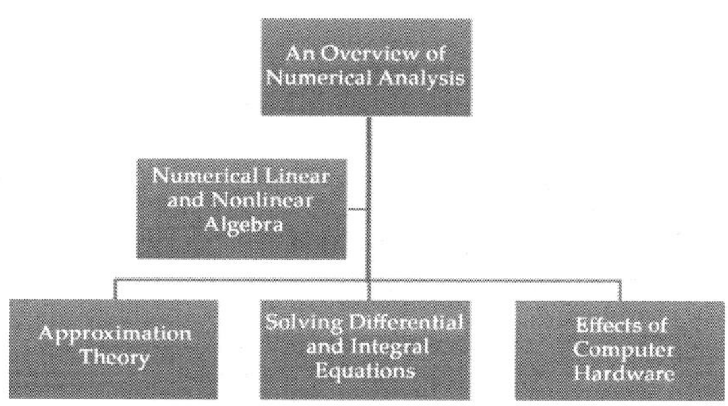

Figure 2.4. An overview of numerical analysis.

Some of the categories of the mathematical theory concerning numerical analysis are discussed as follows, taking into consideration that there is usually an excessive overlap between the listed areas (Figure 2.4).

2.8.1. Numerical Linear and Nonlinear Algebra

This refers to problems including solution of systems of both linear and nonlinear equations, probably with a significant large number of variables. There are various problems in applied mathematics concerned with solving systems of linear equations, with the linear system arising certainly in some instances and as a part of the solution process in other scenarios.

It is generally seen that linear systems can be written with the help of matrix-vector notation, Ax = b, with A refers to the matrix of coefficients for the system, while x mostly refers to column vector of the unknown variables x1, …, xn, and b a given column vector.

Finding solution to linear systems with number of variables up to 1000 is now conceived straightforward in most cases. For linear systems from small to moderate sized (say *n* less than or equal to 1000), the widely accepted and popular numerical method is Gaussian elimination and its variants.

This method is usually an exactly stated algorithmic variant of the method of elimination of variables which is mostly witnessed by the readers of elementary algebra. In case of larger linear systems, there are a number of approaches relying on the structure of the coefficient matrix A.

Direct methods resulted in having theoretically exact solution x in a limited number of steps, with Gaussian elimination the widely popular method. In preparation, there are multiple inaccuracies in the calculated value of x because of rounding errors in the computation, outcome of limited length of numbers in typical computer arithmetic. Iterative methods are methods based on approximation which create a sequence of approximating solutions of rising accuracy.

Linear systems can be classified according with respect to many properties and characteristics (e.g., A may be symmetric about its main diagonal), and specialized methods have been primarily designed for getting solution to problems coupled with these special properties.

It is often seen that nonlinear problems are treated numerically by lessening them to a sequence of linear problems. As a simple but noteworthy example, let's take into notice the problem of solving a nonlinear equation f (x) = 0. Approximate the graph of y = f (x) by the tangent line at a point x (0) near the wanted root, and make use the root of the tangent line in a way to get approximation of root of the original nonlinear function f (x).

This resulted in introduction of Newton's method for root finding:

$$x^{(k+1)} = x^{(k)} - \frac{f(x^{(k)})}{f'(x^{(k)})}, \qquad k = 0,1,2,\ldots$$

This further resulted in simplifying the handling systems of nonlinear equations. Let f (x) = 0 denote a system of n nonlinear equations in n unknowns x1,…, xn. Newton's method for solving this system is given by.

$$x^{(k+1)} = x^{(k)} + \delta^{(k)}$$

$$f'\left(x^{(k)}\right)\delta^{(k)} = -f\left(x^{(k)}\right), \quad 0,1,2,\ldots$$

In this, f (x) is the Jacobian matrix of f (x), and the second equation is a linear system of order n.

It is worth noticing that there are number of other approaches that can be used in solving nonlinear systems, majority of these are relied upon using few types of approximation using linear functions. One important connected class of problems arise under the category of optimization. Given a real-valued function f (x) with x a vector of unknowns, it is possible to get a value of x which minimizes f (x).

In some scenarios, x can be allowed to vary freely, and in other scenarios, there are restrictions on the values of x that can be contemplated. These kinds problems are of recurrent in nature especially in business applications.

2.8.2. Approximation Theory

It is worth noticing that this category includes the approximation of functions and methods dependent on using such approximations. While evaluating a function f (x) with x a complex or real number, it is important to keep in mind that a calculator or computer can do only a limited number of operations.

In addition to this, these operations refer to the basic arithmetic operations of subtraction, addition, division, and multiplication, accompanied with comparison operations such as determining whether $x>y$ is true or false.

Having the four basic arithmetic operations in hand, one can evaluate polynomials

P (x) = a0 + a1x +... + anxn

and rational functions that are polynomials divided by polynomials. Comprising the comparison operations, it is possible to evaluate variety of rational or polynomials functions on different sets of real numbers x.

The evaluation of all other functions, for instance f (x) = √x or 2x, can be reduced to the evaluation of a rational or polynomial function that guesses the given function with adequate correctness. All function evaluations on computers and calculators can be attained with this approach.

This topic is known by the name approximation theory, and it is a fully matured area of mathematics.

One popular method of approximation referred as interpolation. Consider being given a set of points (xi, yi), i = 0, 1,…., n, and then finding a polynomial (*) which satisfies p (xi) = yi, i = 0, 1,…., n. The polynomial p (x) referred to interpolate the specified data points.

It is possible to perform interpolation with functions other than polynomials (although these are the widely recognized segment of interpolating functions), with important cases being trigonometric polynomials, rational functions, and spline functions. It is important to note that interpolation has a number of applications.

If a function is known only at a discrete set of data points x0,…., xn, with yi = f (xi), then interpolation can allow to lengthen the definition to nearby points x. If n encompass large numbers, then spline functions are desirable to polynomials for this objective.

Spline functions are basically smooth piecewise polynomial functions having restricted oscillation, and they are widely used in statistics, computer graphics as well as in other applications.

Most numerical methods for the calculation of derivatives and integrals of a given function f (x) are relied on interpolation. Started by the formulation of an interpolating function p (x) that approximates f (x), usually a polynomial, and then differentiate and integrate p (x) to estimate the derivative or corresponding integral of f (x).

2.8.3. Solving Differential and Integral Equations

It is important to note that majority of the mathematical models used in the natural sciences and engineering are dependent on ODEs, integral equations as well as PDEs. For these equations, the numerical methods are basically of two types: The first type is concerned with the approximation of unknown function in the equation by a simpler function, usually a piecewise polynomial or polynomial function, preferring it to please the actual equation approximately. Among the some popular one of such methods is the finite element method for solving PDEs. The second one of numerical method estimates the integrals or derivatives in the equation of interest, commonly solving approximately for the solution function at a discrete set of points.In majority of the cases, preliminary value problems for PDEs and ODEs are solved in this way, and the numerical procedures are generally known by the name finite difference methods, primarily for historical reasons. Majority of the numerical methods for getting solution to integral and differential equations include both approximation theory and the solution of quite nonlinear and large linear systems.

2.8.4. Effects of Computer Hardware

It is generally seen that majority of numerical computation is carried out on digital computers, and their properties and structure affect the structure of numerical algorithms, particularly while finding solution to lengthy linear systems.

First and foremost, it is important to have comprehensive understanding of computer arithmetic. Historically, computer arithmetic varied to a greater extent between different producers of computers, and this was a primary cause of major variety of problems while trying to write software which could be easily transferred from one computer to another.

This has been largely backed by growth of the Institute for Electronic and Electrical Engineering (IEEE) standard for computer floating-point arithmetic. It was found that majority of small computer producers have adopted to this standard, and most dominant computer players have also done the same.

For problems of large scale, particularly in numerical linear algebra, it is noteworthy to notice how the elements of a vector x and an array A are stored in memory. Gaining an understanding of this may conducive to much rapid transfer of numbers from the memory into the arithmetic registers of the computer, resulting in efficient and effective programs. One topic of similar kind is that of pipelining.

This technique has been widely used whereby the implementation of computer operations are sometimes overlapped, resulting in faster execution. It is generally seen that machines having similar basic clock speed can have very distinctive program execution times because of variation in pipelining and differences in the way memory is stored and retrieved.

It is generally seen that most computers of present time possess sequential ability in their operation, but parallel computers are much more in use. Some parallel computers have processors which are not dependent on others, thus accessing the memory of only their own computer memory (shared memory parallel computers), whereas other parallel computers have separate memory for each processor (distributed memory parallel computers).

Another category of parallelism is to make use of pipelining of vector arithmetic operations. Some parallel machines refer to a grouping of all or some of these patterns of memory pipelining and storage. With all parallel machines, the category of a numerical algorithm should be altered in a way to make best use of the parallelism.

2.9. MODERN APPLICATIONS AND COMPUTER SOFTWARE IN NUMERICAL METHODS

Mathematical modeling and numerical analysis have become critical in many parts of modern life. Complicated numerical analysis software is being integrated in prevalent software packages, for instance, spreadsheet programs, making it possible for many people to execute modeling even when actual mathematics knowledge involved in the process is unknown.

This requires creating proficient, steady, and precise numerical analysis software; and it necessitates planning problem solving environments (PSE) in which it is comparatively straight forward to model a given situation.

The PSE for a specified area of problem is primarily relied on excellent theoretical mathematical models, made available to the user through an appropriate graphical user interface. Such software tools are properly developed in some areas, for instance, computer aided design (CAD) of structures, while other segments are still struggling with some fundamental problems of creating precise mathematical models and accompanying tools for their solution, e.g., atmospheric modeling.

2.9.1. Some Application Areas

Computer aided manufacturing (CAM) and CAD are two imperative areas within engineering, and some quite complex PSEs have been developed for CAM/CAD. A huge range of numerical analysis is intricate in the mathematical models that should be resolved. All these models are dependent on the basic Newtonian laws of mechanics; there are a huge list of possible models, and research has been continued on designing such models for a prolonged period of time.One essential CAD topic is that of modeling the dynamics of moving mechanical systems. The mathematical model includes systems of both ordinary algebraic equations and differential equations (generally nonlinear).The numerical analysis of these mixed systems, known by the name differential-algebraic systems, is fairly challenging but essential to being able to model moving mechanical systems. It is generally seen that formation of simulators for planes, cars, and other vehicles requires solving differential-algebraic systems on a real time basis.

Atmospheric modeling is prerequisite for simulating the behavior of the Earth's atmosphere, to comprehend the probable outcome of human activities on present atmosphere. There is need for introduction of a large number of variables.

These include the velocity v (x, y, z, t) in the atmosphere at time t, position (x, y, z), and the temperature T (x, y, z, t), and the pressure p (x, y, z, t). Moreover, there is need for gaining an understanding about various chemicals present in the atmosphere and their interactions, including numerous chemical pollutants, ozone, carbon dioxide, and others hazardous elements.

The underlying equations for studying p (x, y, z, t), v (x, y, z, t), and T (x, y, z, t) are PDEs; and the chemical kinetic interactions of the several chemicals are defined using some rather challenging ODEs. It is generally seen that many types of numerical analysis procedures are being used in atmospheric modeling, comprising numerical solution of differential equations and computational fluid mechanics.

It is important to note that most modern-day businesses make use of optimization methods in a way to determine how to allocate resources more effectively and efficiently. These embrace problems such as scheduling, inventory control, how best to trace storage and manufacturing facilities, investment strategies, and others. The numerical analysis of optimization problems has been discussed earlier in this section.

2.9.2. Computer Software

Software that are concerned with implementation of common numerical analysis procedures play very important role. In case it is required to be shared with many users, it needs to be perfect, consistent, and efficient at the same time. In addition, it needs to be written in such a way that it possesses the ability of portability between different computers, which the ability to move from one computer to another.Beginning around 1970, there have been a significant number of research initiative undertaken and sponsored by government with the objective to enhance the quality numerical analysis software, especially in vulnerable areas.One more recent example of such a project is the LAPACK project that carries state-of-the-art programs for fundamental problems in numerical linear algebra. Two imperative online numerical analysis libraries that includes majority of these lengthy scale numerical analysis programming projects are available at internet sites shared as follows:

Name	URL	Location
Netlib	www.netlib.org	Oak Ridge National Laboratory
GAMS	gams.nist.gov	National Institute of Standards and Technology

It is worth noticing that one of the most widely recognized programming languages for implementing numerical analysis methods continues to be Fortran, and it changes continuously from time after assessing the current and future needs and demands, with Fortran 95 being the most modern and accepted standard.

Not only this, there are various other languages that play very important role. Some of the important ones are Java, C, C++ Other essential approach that contributes in providing programming tools and numerical analysis programs has been to create higher level PSE that entails programming, numerical, and graphical tools, comprising some fairly complicated numerical analysis tools in order to address some fundamental problems.

Popular ones among them is MATLAB (c The Math works, Inc.), a commercial package that has been widely accepted among large number of users to do numerical computing. For analytical mathematics computing, there are basically two imperative commercial packages: Mathematica (c Wolfram Research, Inc.), and Maple (c Waterloo Maple, Inc.).

2.10. NUMERICAL METHODS WITH POWERFUL TOOLS

It is well known that the numerical methods play very important role and with the help of it, many problems can be solved that would otherwise be insoluble. In the past, numerically solving of problems requires huge amount of knowledge of numerical problems and programming.

Various programming languages such as Basic, Fortran, C, and Pascal have been extensively used by engineers and scientists, but they are usually complicated to program and to debug. Some of the advanced modern software that are now easily available has gone a long way to address such challenges. Maple, Matlab, MathCAD, and Mathematica for instance, are relatively more manageable, as most of the operations have been modularized, such that the programmer now can most easily observed what actually is going on.

However, some spreadsheet programs enabled scientists and engineers with very powerful tools. Two widely recognized and popular ones in these lectures are Open Office.org Calc and Microsoft Excel. Spreadsheets are much more intuitive as compared to using high-level languages, and it provide every person the opportunity to use it because of its simplicity and easily accessibility to a certain level. Yet often there are many users that do not know how to translate powerful numerical procedures into spreadsheet calculations.

In this section, the primary objective is to present the theory of the most valuable numerical methods and to demonstrate how to implement them, ordinarily in a spreadsheet, but sometimes also in a programming language. In some scenarios, spreadsheets are not considered satisfactory for computations of large-scale operations.

The two spreadsheets that are mentioned are:

- **Microsoft Excel**: It is one of the most popularly known and widely used spreadsheet. Some of its efficacy for computations of numerical problem comes from pair of modules, *Solver*, and *Goal Seek*, which avert the need for much computations and programming. *Goal Seek*, is very straight forward in its application, but it is limited in its use.

With the help of Goal Seek, it is easy to solve a single equation, however, intricate or however, many spreadsheet cells are involved, whether the equation is nonlinear or linear. While comparatively on the other hand, *Solver* is much more powerful. It was primarily designed for optimization problems, where one need to find values of a number of different parameters such that some quantity is curtailed, usually the summation of errors of a number of equations.

With this tool, it is easy to find such optimal solutions, or solutions having 1 or many equations, even if they are of nonlinear in nature. In this section, the primary objective is to simplify many procedures. It may seem to be annoying, however, that solver is not inevitably installed. For this, one need to open Excel, then click on the Tools tab. In case Solver is not present there (as the case with some excel version), then there is need to click on Add-ins, and proceed to install it.

- **OpenOffice.org Calc**: Open Office refers to a shareware version of Microsoft Office, having a word processor, presentation program, spreadsheet, and drawing program; it is possible to download from the site, http://www.openoffice.org/. The spreadsheet is known by the name called *Calc*.

It is important to note that it has most of the features of *Excel*, including *Goal Seek*, but during the time of writing, it still does not have a broader version of nonlinear of *Solver*, although one is in the development phase.

As far as this course is concerned, it is of major disadvantage. While it is possible to modified it to a greater extent, in this section the major focus will be on Excel only and will use that as a generic name for the two programs.

2.10.1. Accuracy

Accuracy, errors, and computer arithmetic

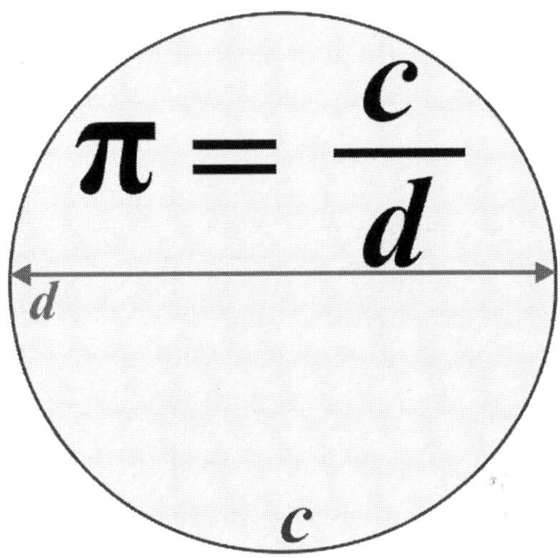

Figure 2.5. Elementary algebra.

Source: Image by Wikipedia.

It is worth noticing that excel possess the ability to stores and calculates with 15-digit accuracy. This is corresponding to duo exactness in some programming languages, and is correct enough that majority of calculations will not bear hefty loss of accuracy.

Whenever numbers are stored via machine, a minimal error is often expected. *Excel* can store numbers in the range from 2-1024≈ 10-308. In case, a number is less than the required minimum, then it stores it as 0, if it is greater than the maximum, then it records it as an overflow in the form #NUM! Unlike the languages of programming, *Excel* does not distinguish between floating point and integers numbers

2.10.2. Rounding

- Excel often shows numbers approximated to the accuracy of the display. For instance, if you evaluate 2/3 and the cell has been configured to show up to 4 decimal places, it will look like 0.6667.
- In case, there is need to approximate a number, there is a function called ROUND (decimal, number, places) which rounds a number up to a certain number of decimal places. In case, the decimal places is 0, then the number should be rounded to the closest integer, that are often important in programming.

Example: ROUND (3:14159; 3) gives 3.142.

2.10.3. Errors

Blunders: These are actually not errors, but are mistakes, for instance, inputting the wrong digit.

Errors in the Model: A mathematical model in environmental and civil engineering does not typically exemplify all facet of a real problem, such as the negligence of turbulence in hydraulics.

Errors in the Data: It is generally seen that majority of data from a physical problem include uncertainties or errors, because of restricted accuracy of the measuring device.

Truncation Error: This is the error that usually occurs when a restricted process is curtailed before one has reached the limiting value such as when a countless series is shattered off after a finite number of terms.

Example: Computing sin x from the first three terms of its power series expansion x-x3/3! + x5/5!

Round-off Error: It is the error that usually occur because of the narrow accuracy of the computer, and a probability of round-off error occurs whenever numbers are stored and function of arithmetic operations.

2.11. CONCLUSION

In the end, it is concluded that numerical methods provide much needed oxygen to various complicated problems. In order to get the accurate and exact result from numerical methods, there is need to grab comprehensive understanding of the same and the doer should follow a complete set of procedures for finding solution to a problem, however, a meager amount of error is possible. In the current time frame, role of numerical methods is paramount as it allows to solve real-life mathematical, engineering, and physical problems.It is generally seen that there are many programming languages such as Basic, Fortran, C, and Pascal that are widely used by engineers and scientists for finding solution to numerical problems. But these cannot be used by general public. For them, latest, and easy to use software available in the market that perform the same operation at minimal cost and time.

There are different types of software available in the market for numerical problems, but they should be used after analyzing the proper need and requirement. As some of them comes at a huge cost, therefore it is important to engage in decision making before taking any decision.

REFERENCES

1. (2009). Introduction to Numerical Analysis. [ebook] Available at: http://www.math.iitb.ac.in/~baskar/book.pdf (accessed on 4 June 2020).
2. (2014). Numerical Methods. [ebook] Available at: http://vmm.math.uci.edu/ODEandCM/PDF_Files/ChapterFirstPages/First38PagesOFChapter5.pdf (accessed on 4 June 2020).
3. (2020). An Introduction to Programming and Numerical Methods in MATLAB. [ebook] Available at: https://www.math.unipd.it/~mrrusso/Didattica/NA-Yaounde/Manual.pdf (accessed on 4 June 2020).
4. (2020). Numerical Analysis. [ebook] Available at: https://web.njit.edu/~jiang/math614/atkinson1.pdf (accessed on 4 June 2020).
5. (2020). Numerical Solution Methods for Engineering Analysis. [ebook] Available at: https://www.sjsu.edu/me/facultystaff/faculty/tai-ran-hsu/Chapter%2010%20Numerical%20solution%20methods.pdf (accessed on 4 June 2020).
6. (2020). Properties of Numerical Methods. [ebook] Available at: https://www.mathematik.uni-dortmund.de/~kuzmin/cfdintro/lecture9.pdf (accessed on 4 June 2020).
7. Alobaid, F., Epple, B., Leithner, R., Müller, H., Zindler, H., Ponweiser, K., & Walter, H., (2020). Numerical Methods. [online] Springer Link. Available at: https://link.springer.com/chapter/10.1007/978-3-7091-4855-6_3 (accessed on 4 June 2020).
8. Bukiet, L., Pelesko, J., Li, X., & Sachdev, P., (2020). A Characteristic Based Numerical Method with Tracking for Nonlinear Wave Equations. [online] www.sciencedirect.com. Available at: https://www.sciencedirect.com/science/article/pii/0898122196000193 (accessed on 4 June 2020).
9. Bulatov, M., & Machkhina, M., (2006). Features of Behavior of Numerical Methods for Solving Volterra Integral Equations of the Second Kind. [online] springer.com. Available at: https://link.springer.com/article/10.1134/S0965542514030026 (accessed on 4 June 2020).
10. Chasnov, J. R., (2020). Numerical Methods. [ebook] Available at: https://www.math.ust.hk/~machas/numerical-methods.pdf (accessed on 4 June 2020).
11. En.wikipedia.org. (2020). Numerical Analysis. [online] Available at: https://en.wikipedia.org/wiki/Numerical_analysis#History (accessed on 4 June 2020).

12. Encyclopedia.com. (2020). Numerical Methods | Encyclopedia.com. [online] Available at: https://www.encyclopedia.com/computing/dictionaries-thesauruses-pictures-and-press-releases/numerical-methods (accessed on 4 June 2020).
13. Epperson, J. F., (2020). An Introduction to Numerical Methods and Analysis. [ebook] John Wiley & Sons, Inc. Available at: https://perhuaman.files.wordpress.com/2014/07/metodos-numericos.pdf (accessed on 4 June 2020).
14. Epperson, J. F., (2020). An Introduction to Numerical Methods and Analysis. [ebook] Available at: https://pdfs.semanticscholar.org/6d50/92f83a8c2575e16764d99efc66e0a7ed0f82.pdf?_ga=2.199174191.1824666058.1587489224-874659400.1587379689 (accessed on 4 June 2020).
15. Epperson, J., (2020). An Introduction to Numerical Methods and Analysis. [online] Semanticscholar.org. Available at: https://www.semanticscholar.org/paper/An-Introduction-to-Numerical-Methods-and-Analysis-Epperson/a2d69e0f00258baddc67854243af672fa3f209a6 (accessed on 4 June 2020).
16. Fenton, J. D, (2002). Numerical Methods. [ebook] Available at: http://johndfenton.com/Lectures/Numerical-Methods/Numerical-Methods.pdf (accessed on 4 June 2020).
17. Johndfenton.com. (2020). Numerical Method. [online] Available at: http://johndfenton.com/Lectures/Numerical-Methods/Numerical-Methods.pdf (accessed on 4 June 2020).
18. Learn.canvas.net. (2020). Introduction to Numerical Methods-Part 1 of 2. [online] Available at: https://learn.canvas.net/courses/1065 (accessed on 4 June 2020).
19. Research Gate, (2020). A Notebook on Numerical Methods. [online] Available at: https://www.researchgate.net/publication/287209798_A_Notebook_on_Numerical_Methods (accessed on 4 June 2020).
20. Research Gate, (2020). An Introduction to Numerical Methods for the Solution of Partial Differential Equations. [online] Available at: https://www.researchgate.net/publication/266603075_An_Introduction_to_Numerical_Methods_for_the_Solutions_of_Partial_Differential_Equations (accessed on 4 June 2020).
21. ResearchGate, (2020). Numerical Methods with Algorithms and

Programs. [online] Available at: https://www.researchgate.net/publication/283317685_Numerical_Methods_with_algorithms_and_programs (accessed on 4 June 2020).

22. Saeed, R. K., (2020). Introduction to Numerical Analysis. [online] ResearchGate. Available at: https://www.researchgate.net/publication/280311354_Introduction_to_Numerical_Analysis (accessed on 4 June 2020).
23. Sciencedirect.com. (2020). Numerical Method: An Overview | ScienceDirect Topics. [online] Available at: https://www.sciencedirect.com/topics/engineering/numerical-method (accessed on 4 June 2020).
24. Scribd, (2020). Significance ofNumerical Methods | Numerical Analysis | Mathematical Model. [online] Available at: https://www.scribd.com/document/245648457/Significance-of-Numerical-Methods (accessed on 4 June 2020).
25. The James Lind Library, (2020). The Introduction of Numerical Methods to Assess the Effects of Medical Interventions During the 18th Century: A Brief History.-The James Lind Library. [online] Available at: https://www.jameslindlibrary.org/articles/the-introduction-of-numerical-methods-to-assess-the-effects-of-medical-interventions-during-the-18th-century-a-brief-history/ (accessed on 4 June 2020).
26. www.sjsu.edu. (2020). Numerical Solution Methods for Engineering Analysis. [online] Available at: https://www.sjsu.edu/me/facultystaff/faculty/tai-ran-hsu/Chapter%2010%20Numerical%20solution%20methods.pdf (accessed on 4 June 2020).

CHAPTER
3

CLASS AND OBJECTS: IMPORTANT ASPECTS OF PROGRAMMING

CONTENTS

This chapter brings forward the important aspects of class and objects. After introducing the concept of object-oriented programming, this chapter explains the basic concepts of class and objects.

Various types of classes and objects that are used in the object-oriented programming languages such as C++, Java, and Python are extensively discussed in this chapter.

Later in this chapter, classes, and objects in C++, Java, and Python and the differences between classes and objects are explained in this chapter. This chapter also brings forward the various syntax and sample programs that are used to declare classes and objects in the various programming languages.

3.1. INTRODUCTION TO OBJECT-ORIENTED PROGRAMMING

Object-oriented programming, or it is also known as OOP, is defined as an approach to problem solving where all calculations are done by the use of an objects. An object is defined as a component of a program that knows how to perform specific actions and how to interact with the other components of the program. Objects are defined as the fundamental units of object-oriented programming (OOP).

A person is a simple example of an object. Logically, one would be expecting a person to have a name.

This is considered a property of the person. Also, one could expect that a person would be capable of doing something, like driving or walking. This is considered as a method of the person.

It has to be noted that code in OOP is organized around the objects. Once an individual has the objects, they can interact with one another to make something happen.

Let's say there is a need to have a program where an individual gets into a car and he or she drives the car from A to B. One would begin by describing the objects, like an individual and a car. That consists of methods: an individual knows how to drive a car.

On the other hand, a car knows what it is like to be driven. Once the objects are present, one brings these objects together so the individual can get into the car and drive the car from A to B (Figure 3.1).

Figure 3.1. Object-oriented programming languages use classes and objects as important element in the programs.

Source: Image by Wikimedia Commons.

Object-oriented programming (OOP) is defined as a style of programming that pays attention on making use of the objects in order to design and build applications. For instance, one would have a cost object, a status object, and also, there is a client object among others, in a project management application.

All these objects in a project management application would work together (and with various other objects) in order to provide the functionality that an individual want their project management application to have.

Many applications are developed with the help of object-oriented programming (OOP). These applications may be simple and complex applications, games, and business applications, desktop, and mobile applications. It is the developers who choose to program in the object-oriented paradigm.

This is because the appropriate or correct use of objects makes it very easy and simple to build, maintain, as well as upgrade an application. In addition to it, the development of an application with the help of objects that have been tested helps in increasing the reliability of the application.

A class is defined as a template for defining objects in object-oriented terminology. It indicates the types and names of variables that are in an object, and the "methods." These methods are the procedures for operating on those variables. In object-oriented terminology, a class can be thought of as a "type."

Objects being a "variable" of that type. It has to be noted that multiple objects, or examples of a class can be created in a single HLU program, just as an individual declare multiple variables of the similar type in any program.

For instance, the TextItem class is defined as a template that is used to create an object that involves text string. This object will have a set of text attributes like size, font, and color. If the values of the object variables is--resources--in a particular way then the TextItem object "Hello World" can be created. All the resources that are available for objects of the TextItem class consists of the text string (in this scenario, "Hello World"), the color of the characters, the type of font, the line width of the characters, the size of the characters, etc.

Therefore, a TextItem object is an instance of the TextItem class. It has a set of values that is allocated to the related resources. If required, a second TextItem object can also be created with the help of a new set of resource values like: "THIS IS ALSO A TEXTITEM OBJECT."

3.2. UNDERSTANDING CLASSES AND OBJECTS

3.2.1. Class

It has to be noted that class is defined as a concept. The object is the embodiment of that concept. There is a need to have a class before the creation of an object. So, let's suppose that there is a need to use an individual in the program. In this case, there is the need to describe the individual and have the individual perform something.

A class that is known as 'individual' would provide a blueprint for what an individual actually looks like and what an individual can do. There is a need to create an object in order to make use of an individual in the program. The individual class is used to create an object of the type 'individual.' Now one can describe this individual and also, have the individual to perform something.

Classes plays a very important role in programming. Let's suppose there is the need to use not just a single individual but 100 individuals. One can make use of the same individual class to create 100 objects of the type 'individual' instead of describing every single individual in detail from scratch. Still, there is a need to give each individual a name and other properties, but the basic structure of what an individual look like is the same.

It has to be noted that it is a user-defined data type. This holds its own data members as well as member functions. These data members and member functions can be accessed and can be used by creating an instance of that class. It has to be noted that a C++ class is just like a blueprint for an object.

Take an example of the class of Cars. There may be various care that are having different names and brand but all of these cares will have some of properties in common such as all of these cars will be having 4 wheels, the speed Limit, Mileage range and many other properties. In this scenario, car is the class and the speed limit of the car, its wheels, mileage are their properties.

- A Class is considered as a user defined data-type which is having data members as well as member functions.
- Data members are considered as the data variables and member functions are considered as the functions that are used in order to manipulate these variables. And, together these data members and member functions described the properties as well as the behavior of the objects in a Class.
- In the example of class Car that is mentioned above, the speed limit of the car, its mileage etc. will be the data member and member functions can be apply the brakes of the car, increase speed etc.

3.2.2. Objects

An object is defined as a self-contained component in the terms of programming. This component consists of properties as well as methods that are required in order to make a certain kind of data useful. The properties of object are what the object is knows as and the methods of the objects are what it can do.

The project management application that is mentioned above consists of a cost object, a status object and a client object, among others. The current status of the project would be one of the properties of the status object. There is a method that could help in updating that status in a status object.

The properties of the client object would consist of all the essential details about the client and its methods are able to change them. The cost object would have methods that are required to assess the cost of the project. This cost is based on hourly rate, hours worked, cost of the materials and fees.

Apart from providing the functionality of the application, methods also helps in ensuring that the data of an object is used properly by running checks for the particular type of data that is being used. In addition to it, they also allow for the actual execution of tasks to be hidden and for specific operations to be standardized across various kinds of objects.

From an object-oriented perspective, objects are defined as the basic building blocks of applications. There will be various objects of different types that will be used in the development of any application. Each different kind of object comes from a particular class of that type.

3.2.3. Class Versus Object

It has been observed that there are many individuals who get confused by the difference between class and object. The difference between class and object is simple and it is also conceptual. A class is considered as a template for objects. The properties of the object are defined by a class. This includes a valid range of values, and a default value (Figure 3.2).

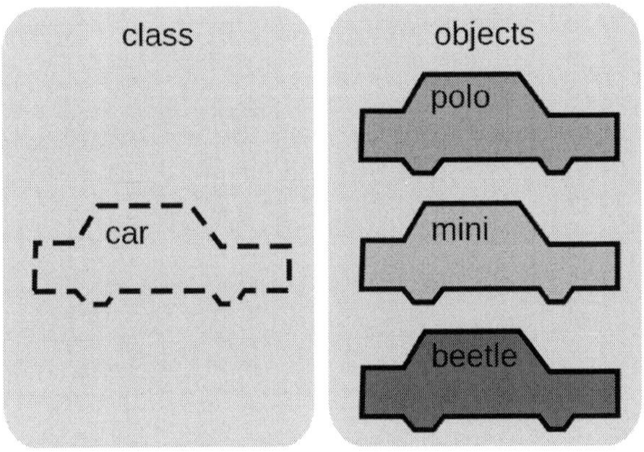

Figure 3.2. Basic example highlighting the difference between class and objects.

Source: Image by Wikimedia commons.

In addition to describing the properties of the object, a class also describes the object behavior. An object is considered as a member or an "instance" of a class. An object has a state, a state in which all the properties of objects have values that are either explicitly defined or the values are defined by default settings.

3.2.4. Derived Classes and Inheritance

It is convenient at times to develop a class that shares the properties with the other class but yet it is different from the original one. The new class that is created derives the properties from an existing class but it has to be noted that the new class also extends or includes some of its own properties. This new class is known as a "derived class." In addition to it, this new class is said to "inherit" its properties as well as the functionality from the original class.

For instance, let's suppose that the original class is a class that is known as Box. This class id defined to have two properties. These properties are side length, and color. The valid values for these properties in the Box class are:

0. <= side length <= 21., default= 6.

Color is pink or black, default = pink.

If there is the creation of an instance of the Box class or, in other terms, an object that is in the Box class, it will have the properties of Box class (that is side length, and color). Unless the values of the properties are explicitly set, these will be defined as the default

Now take an example that there is the need to create a box object that is filled instead of the hollow boxes that are created by the use of Box class template. In spite of make an entirely new template that consists of many of the similar properties of the Box class, a new class can be derived and also the functionality of the derived class can be extended as necessary in order to create a class that described the filled box objects.

The name of the derived class is FilledBox. Since this class is derived from the Box class, it will inherit all the properties that were in the Box class automatically. These properties include, side length, and color. However, there is a need to add a new property which is known as fill with possible values of "on" or "off" and a default value of "on" in order to create boxes that are filled. Any of the new objects that are created that are in the Filled Box class will be drawn as filled boxes until and unless the fill property is set to "off.."

A class is defined as a blueprint or template or it can also be called set of instructions that is used to build a particular type of object. It has to be noted that every object is created from a class. Every single class should be designed as well as programmed in order to achieve one, and just one, thing. Many classes are used in order to create a complete application. This is because each class is designed and programmed to have just one responsibility,

A specific object that is built from a specific class is an example. It is assigned to a reference variable that is used in order to access all of the properties as well as methods of instance. When a new instance is made, the process is known as instantiation and is usually done by the use of the new keyword.

Let's suppose about the instances, classes, and instantiation such as baking a cake. A class is just like a recipe for chocolate cake. The recipe of the cake itself is not a cake. One cannot eat the recipe (or at least one would not want to). If one correctly does what the recipe asks to do (instantiate it) then an edible cake is made. That edible cake is considered an instance of the chocolate cake class.

Many cakes can be bakes as one would like to by the use of the same recipe of chocolate cake. In the similar way, many instances of a class can be instantiated as one would like. For example, there is the need to bake three cakes for three friends who all have birthday and anniversary at the same date, but they are of different ages. In order to bake three different cakes for friends, there is a need of some way to keep the track of which cake is for which friend so the correct number of candles can be put on the cakes.

Writing the names of each friend on the cake is a simple solution. Reference variables also work in a same manner. A unique name is provided for each instance of a class by reference variable. One make use of the reference variable it is assigned to in order to work with a particular instance.

3.2.5. Super Classes and Subclasses

Subclass of the original class is the other way to refer to a derived class. Super class is defined as the class from which the subclass is derived. For instance, View class is the super class of the Text Item class, in the HLU library.One thing that all the View subclasses have in common is that all these classes can be used in order to create graphical objects. Some of the other subclasses of the View class consists of Vector Plot, XyPlot, Tick Mark, Legend, Streamline Plot, Map Plot, Contour Plot, Title, and Label Bar. Base class is defined as the super class of all subclasses.

It has to be noted that often the super classes cannot be instantiated directly. For example, one cannot create a View object or a Base object. The responsibility of these super classes is to describe the common methods as well as resources that, through inheritance, are available to their subclasses automatically. For instance, the non-instantiable Workstation super class described a resource, wkColorMap. It consists of a list of presently allocated colors.

The PSWorkstation class is used to output PostScript. It is defined as a subclass of Workstation. Also, the wkColorMap resource can be accessed by

PSWorkstation object. As a matter of fact, all the resources that are defined by the Workstation class are available to a PSWorkstation object. In fact, these resources are available to objects that are belonging to any subclass of Workstation, like the XWorkstation class or the Ncgm Workstation class.

3.2.6. Mixed Classes

A mixed class is the other way that is used to combine the functionality from the other classes into a new class. All the properties of other classes are managed by this mixed class. This mixed class only make use of a subset of the functionality of a class. On the other hand, a derived class make use of the complete set of functionalities of its super classes and it generally extends this functionality.

For instance, suppose there is one more class in addition to the Box class that is known as Text. The Text class has a single property, which is known as string. It has a default value of "hello world."

A mixed class could be created that would manage these two simple classes to create a box object with text. The new class is known as Textbox. In this scenario, it will make use of all the properties from both of the classes from which it is created. It has been observed that in most of the cases, the mixed class only make use of a subset of the properties from these classes. The object that is in the TextBox class would consists of the following properties, these properties includes side length, string, and color.

The XyPlot class is considered as an example of an HLU mixed class. This class combines the functionality of the Title class and Tick Mark class, among others. Since both tick marks and titles are involved in an XyPlot object (both of them are also available as HLU classes), it is more effective to have the XyPlot class to manage all these properties instead of using its own code and properties in order to provide redundant functionality.

3.2.7. Composite Classes

Mixed classes are called "composite classes" in the HLU library. The boxes which are having a heavy outline are composite classes in the class hierarchy chart. For instance, if an individual click on the box Plot Manager class, he or she will see that it has as composite class members the Title, Label Bar, Legend, and Tick Mark classes. Composite classes helps in enabling access to at least one of the subsets of the resources of their composite class members.

It has to be noted that the composite class members can be nested. For instance, it has been observed that the Contour Plot class consists of the Plot Manager as a composite class member. Thus, all the composite class members of the Plot Manager are made 3 available to the Contour Plot class.

If a Contour Plot object is created, one have access not just to the resources of the Contour Plot and its super classes, but one can also have access to resources of the Plot Manager and the composite class members of the Plot Manager, that includes, Title, Legend, Tick Mark, and Label Bar. In other terms, there is the only need to create one object in the HLU program in order to have the efficient functionality of an entire tree of composite class members.

3.2.8. User Creatable Objects

Only those objects that are belonging to certain classes can be created directly in a user program. On the other hand, the yellow boxes denote these user-instantiable classes in the class hierarchy chart. The other classes are classified under one of the four categories:

Non-instantiable super classes like View and Base

Classes that are designed and programmed to function just as composite class members, like Plot Manager and subclasses of the Transformation class

The classes that are having just one instance, like Workspace and Error. When the HLU library is initialized, they are instantiated automatically

Those Classes that are instantiated by specific objects on behalf of the client for a specific purpose. At the present times, these classes consists of the XyDataSpec classes and Anno Manager classes

3.2.9. Dynamically Associated Objects

Apart from the class hierarchy as well as composite class relationships, the HLU library is having a mechanism that enables an individual to dynamically associate independently-created View objects. In addition to it, one can also "overlay" Transform class objects on the data space of a plot object.

Also, any View object can be made into an "annotation" of a plot object. The combination of the base plot object, the annotations of base plot object and its overlays, acts like a single object in various ways. In the Plot Manager class module, and in the Anno Manager class module, plot objects, it overlays and its annotations are discussed.

3.3. CLASS HIERARCHY VERSUS INSTANCE HIERARCHY

Other than the class hierarchy of subclasses that is derived from the Base super class, one should be aware of the fact that the HLU library describes an "instance hierarchy" of the objects that are made in the course of implementing an HLU program. It has to be noted that both of hierarchies are totally different, and one should get confused with these two hierarchies.

Whenever an object is created, one must specify the parent of the object as one of the parameters in order to the create call. Therefore, each object that is created is the "child" of some object's parent. The initial parent that is created must be an "application" (App) object.

This initial parent object is known as the "ancestor" of all the objects that are created. Depending on the call that is used to initialize the HLU library, there is the need for an individual to create the object by himself or herself, or in the other case, the library may create the object automatically.

The instance hierarchy is important in the ways that are mentioned below:

- When a parent object is destroyed, all the children of this parent object are destroyed along with it.
- There must be a Workstation class ancestor for a View object. This Workstation class ancestor helps in supplying the view space on which it is drawn.
- The resource database make use of the instance hierarchy in order to determine how resource specifications in the resource files are applied to the specific objects in an HLU program.

3.4. CLASSES AND OBJECTS IN C++

A class is described in C++ by the use of keyword class. This is followed by the name of class. It has to be noted that the body of class is explained inside the curly brackets. The body of the class is terminated by a semicolon at the end.

Declaring Objects: Only the specification for the object is defined when a class is defined. There is no allocation of storage or memory. There is the need to create objects in order to make use of the data and access all those functions that are defined in the class.

Syntax that is used:

Class Name Object Name;

3.4.1. Accessing Data Members and Member Functions

It has been observed that the data members and member functions of class can be accessed by the use of the dot (.") operator with the object. For instance, if abc is the name of object and one need to access the member function with the name printName() then there is the need to write abc. printName().

3.4.1.1. Accessing Data Members

In the similar way that is discussed above, the public data members are also accessed. Though, it has to be noted that the private data members are not allowed to be accessed by the object. Accessing a data member is dependent just on the access control of that data member.

Access modifiers in C++ provided this access control. There exist three access modifiers. These are private, public, and protected.

```
filter_none
edit
play_arrow
brightness_4
// C++ program to demonstrate
// accessing of data members
#include <bits/stdc++.h>
using namespace std;
class Geeks
{
// Access specifier
public:
// Data Members
string geekname;
// Member Functions()
void printname()
```

```
{
cout << "Geekname is: " << geekname;
}
};
int main () {
// Declare an object of class geeks
Geeks obj1;
// accessing data member
obj1.geekname = "Abhi";
// accessing member function
obj1.printname();
return 0;
}
Output:
Geekname is Hercules
```

3.4.1.2. Member Functions in Classes

Basically, there are 2 ways that are used to define a member function:

- Inside class definition; and
- Outside class definition.

There is the need to make use of the scope resolution in order to define a member function outside the class definition that is operator along with the function name and class name.

```
filter_none
edit
play_arrow
brightness_4
// C++ program to demonstrate function
// declaration outside class
#include <bits/stdc++.h>
using namespace std;
class Geeks
```

```
{
public:
string geekname;
int id;
// printname is not defined inside class definition
void printname();
// printid is defined inside class definition
void printed()
{
cout << "Geek id is: " << id;
}
};
// Definition of printname using scope resolution operator::
void Geeks::printname()
{
cout << "Geekname is: " << geekname;
}
int main() {
Geeks obj1;
obj1.geekname = "xyz";
obj1.id=15;
// call printname()
obj1.printname();
cout << endl;
// call printed()
obj1.printed();
return 0;
}
```

Output:

```
Geekname is: xyz
Geek id is: 15
```

It should be noted that all the member functions that are described inside the class definition are by default inline, but any non-class function can be made in line with the help of using keyword in line with them. Inline functions are defined as the actual functions. These functions are copied everywhere at the time of compilation, such as pre-processor macro. These are copied everywhere so that the overhead of function calling is reduced.

It should be noted that the declaration of a friend function is a way that is used to provide private access to a non-member function.

3.4.2. Constructors

Constructors are defined as the special class members. These special class members are called by the compiler at every instance when an object of that particular class is referenced. There is the same name for the constructors as the class and it may be defined inside the class definition or outside the class definition.

Constructors are classified in to three types:

- Default constructors;
- Parameterized constructors; and
- Copy constructors.

filter_none

edit

play_arrow

brightness_4

```
// C++ program to demonstrate constructors
#include <bits/stdc++.h>
using namespace std;
class Geeks
{
public:
int id;
//Default Constructor
Geeks()
{
cout << "Default Constructor called" << endl;
```

```
id=-1;
}
//Parametrized Constructor
Geeks(int x)
{
cout << "Parametrized Constructor called" << endl;
id=x;
}
};
int main () {
// obj1 will call Default Constructor
Geeks obj1;
cout << "Geek id is: " <<obj1.id << endl;
// obj1 will call Parametrized Constructor
Geeks obj2(21);
cout << "Geek id is: " <<obj2.id << endl;
return 0;
}
```

Output:

```
Default Constructor called
Geek id is: -1
Parametrized Constructor called
Geek id is: 21
```

A new object is created by a copy constructor. This new object is the exact copy of the existing object. A default Copy Constructor is provided to all the classes by the compiler.

Syntax that is used:

```
class-name (class-name &){}
```

3.4.3. Destructors

Destructor is the other special member function. This special member function is called by the compiler at the time when the scope of the object ends.

```
filter_none
edit
play_arrow
brightness_4
// C++ program to explain destructors
#include <bits/stdc++.h>
using namespace std;
class Geeks
{
public:
int id;
//Definition for Destructor
~Geeks()
{
cout << "Destructor called for id: " << id <<endl;
}
};
int main()
{
Geeks obj1;
obj1.id=7;
int i = 0;
while (i < 5)
{
Geeks obj2;
obj2.id=i;
i++;
}// Scope for obj2 ends here
return 0;
}// Scope for obj1 ends here
```

Output:

Destructor called for id: 0

Destructor called for id: 1

Destructor called for id: 2

Destructor called for id: 3

Destructor called for id: 4

Destructor called for id: 7

3.5. CLASSES AND OBJECTS IN JAVA

Classes and Objects are defined as the fundamental concepts of Object-Oriented Programming which rotate all around the real-life entities. Java is one of the OOP language.In Java, everything is related with classes and objects, and also with its methods as well as attributes. For instance: a bicycle is an object in a real life. The bicycle has many attributes, like the color of bicycle and its weight, and methods, like drive and brake.Object: There are states and behaviors in objects. For instance, there are many states in cats. These includes name, color, breed, and behaviors such as meowing, eating. An object is the example of a class.Class: A class is defined as a template or the blueprint that defines the behavior or the state that the object of its kind support.

3.5.1. Class in Java Programming

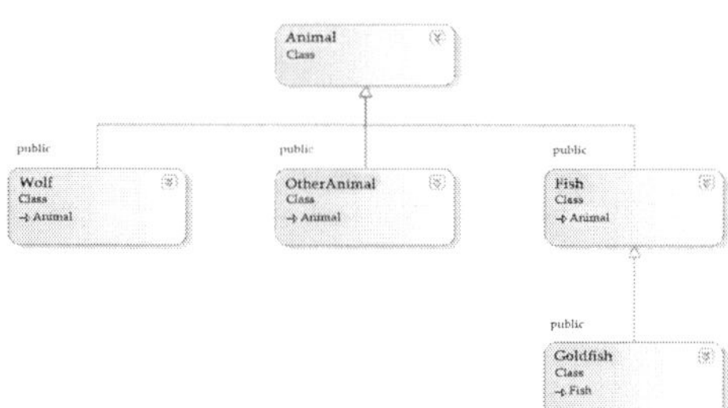

Figure 3.3. An example of class in java programming language.

Source: Image by Wikimedia Commons.

A class is a defined as a user defined blueprint or it is prototype from the help of which the objects are created.

It indicates the set of properties or the methods that are common in all the objects that are of one type. In general term, class declarations can consist of these components, in order (Figure 3.3):

Modifiers: It has to be noted that a class can be public or it has default access (Refer this for details).

Class Name: The name should always start with an initial letter (capitalized by convention).

Super Class (if any): The name of the parent of the class (super class), if there is any, preceded by the keyword extends. Only one parent can be extended by a class.

Interfaces (in case if present): A list of interfaces, that is separated by the commas, is implemented by the class. This only happens if it is preceded by the any keyword implementations. More than one interface can be implemented by a class.

Body: It is the braces { } that surrounds the class body.

It has been observed that in real time applications, there are several kinds of classes that are used like anonymous class, nested classes, lambda expressions.

A class can consists of any of the following types of variable.

- Local variables: The local variables are the variables that are defined inside methods, constructors or blocks. The local variables are usually declared and initialized within the method and the variable will be destroyed when the method has completely executed.
- Instance variables: The kind of variables that exist within a class but are present outside any method are known as the Instance variables. This type of variables is initialized when the class is instantiated. Instance variables can be accessed from inside any method, constructor or blocks of that particular class.
- Class variables: The variables that are declared within a class, outside any method, along with the static keyword are known as Class variables.

3.5.2. Objects in Java Programming

It is the fundamental unit of the Object-oriented Programming. The real-life entities are denoted by the objects. A typical Java program creates many objects which interact with the help of invoking methods. An object contains:

State: Attributes of an object represent the state. The state depicts the properties of an object.

Behavior: The behavior explains the methods of an object. Also, it depicts the response of an object with other objects.

Identity: Identity makes the object unique while enabling one object to interact with the other objects.

Example of an object: dog

Table 3.1. Difference between Class and Objects in Java

Object	**Class**
Object is defined as an instance of a class.	Class is defined as a blueprint or template from which objects are created.
Object is considered as a real-world entity like laptop, bed, mouse, chair, pen, mobile, keyboard, etc.	Class is defined as a group of similar objects.
Object is a physical entity.	Class is a logical entity.
Object is made through new keyword particularly for example, Student s1=new Student ();	Class is declared by the use of class keyword for example, class Student{}
Object is created many times according to the need.	Unlike object, class is declared just once.
When object is created, it allocates memory.	When Class is created, it does not allocate memory.
There are various ways that can be used to create object in java like clone () method, new keyword, new Instance () method, factory method and deserialization.	There is only a single way that is used to define class in java by the use of class keyword.

Source: Table by javapoint.com

3.6. WAYS TO CREATE OBJECT OF A CLASS

In Java programming language, there are four major ways to create objects in the program. Primarily, there is only one way of creating objects in Java program. That is by using new keyword. Apart from using a new keyword, all the other three ways use the new keyword internally in the program.

3.6.1. Using New Keyword

Using a new keyword is the most common and the general way to create object in java. In most of the programs, objects are created by using a new keyword. Below given is an Example that explains how to create an object by using a new keyword:

```
// creating object of class Test
Test t = new Test();
```

3.6.2. Using Class for Name (String Class Name) Method

In Java programming language, there is a pre-defined class in known as java.lang. This package comes with the name Class. The for Name (String Class Name) method returns the Class object that is connected with the class with the given string name.

In this method, a fully qualified and appropriate name must be given for a class. On calling new Instance () method on this Class object returns new instance of the class with the given string name.

```
// creating object of public class Test
// consider class Test present in com.p1 package
Test obj = (Test) Class.forName("com.p1.Test").newInstance();
```

3.6.3. Using Clone () Method

clone() method is present in Object class. It creates and returns a copy of the object.

```
// creating object of class Test
Test t1 = new Test();
// creating clone of above object
Test t2 = (Test)t1.clone();
```

3.6.4. Deserialization

The method or technique of reading an object that is already present in the saved state in a file is known as Deserialization.

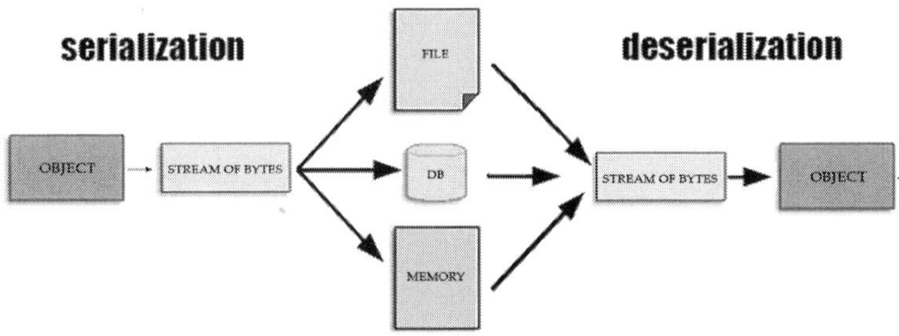

Figure 3.4. An example of serialization and deserialization in Java programming language.

Source: Image by Wikimedia Commons

```
FileInputStream file = new FileInputStream(filename);
ObjectInputStream in = new ObjectInputStream(file);
Object obj = in.readObject();
```

3.7. CREATING MULTIPLE OBJECTS BY ONE TYPE ONLY

In the real-time programming, there is a requirement of different objects that belong to various classes, which belong to different methods. It has been observed that creating a large number of references for storing these objects and classes is not a good practice. Therefore, it is always advised to declare or create a static reference variable. This static reference variable can be put to use whenever there is a need.

By creating a static variable, there is very less wastage of memory. In fact, only a small portion of memory is used for storing a static reference variable. So, there is no need for creating a large number off references that consume larger part of the system memory. As soon as the static variable reference is crated, there are some objects that are not referenced anymore and do not have any significance in the program. These objects will then be destroyed by Garbage Collector of java. Below given is an example:

```
Test T1 = new Test();
T2 = new Test();
```

In the inheritance system, the parent class reference variable is used in order to store a sub-class object. In this case, there is an option to switch into different subclass objects by making use of the same referenced variable. This can be explained with the help of an example:

```
class Animal {}
class Dog extends Animal {}
class Cat extends Animal {}
public class Test
{
// using Dog object
Animal obj = new Dog();
// using Cat object
obj = new Cat();
}
```

3.8. ANONYMOUS OBJECTS IN JAVA PROGRAMMING

There are various objects that are represented in the program but are not stored in any reference variable. These types of objects are known as Anonymous Objects. Anonymous objects might not have any kind of significance in the programs. There are some characteristics of the anonymous objects in the computer programming that make them of some use to the programmers. Some of the major characteristics of anonymous objects are:

- Anonymous objects are used for immediate method calling;
- Just after being called through immediate method calling, the anonymous objects are destroyed; and
- Anonymous objects are extensively used in a number of libraries. For instance, in AWT libraries, the anonymous objects are used to perform a certain number of actions that are relevant to capturing an event such as pressing a key.

In the example mentioned below, when a key, also known as button and referred as the 'btn' in the program, is pressed, an anonymous object of the PhenomHandler class is simple created or declared for just calling the handle method.

```
btn.setOnAction(new PhenomHandler()
{
public void handle(ActionPhenom event)
{
System.out.println("Hello World!");
}
});
```

3.8.1. Source File Declaration Rules

There are some major rules the look into the source file declaration rules. In the Java programming language, these rules hold a great significance and are very essential for the processes of declaring classes, along with importing statements and calling package statements in a source file. The rules for declaring a source file are:

- For a particular source file, there can be only a singular public class;
- There can be a multiple non-public class present for a particular source file;
- The name of the public class and the name of the source file must be same. There should not be any kind of difference in the names of the public class and the source file. For example: the class name is public class Engineer{} then the source file should be as Engineer.java;
- Every source file name should be followed by the extension.java at the end;
- If the class is defined inside a package, then the first statement present in the source file should be same as the package statement;
- In case if there are any import statements present, then these import statements must be written in between the package statement and the class declaration. If there is an absence of package statements, then the source file must have the import statement as its first line;
- All the classes that are present in the source files will implied by all the import and package statements. It becomes a very tedious task to declare different import and/or package statements to different classes in the source file;

- There are different levels of access to the classes. Also, there are a number of classes. Some of the major types of classes are abstract classes, final classes, etc.; and
- In Java programming classes, there are some other classes other than the classes that are mentioned above. Some of the special classes in Java programming language are known as Inner classes and Anonymous classes.

3.8.2. Java Package

Java package is known as the method of categorizing the classes and interfaces. During the phase of developing applications in Java, there are a number of classes and interfaces will be written. Therefore, by dividing different classes and interferes in a number of classes becomes a necessity and makes it easier to run and execute the program.

3.8.3. Import Statements

In Java programming language, if there is a name that is fully qualified, then it becomes easy for the compiler to locate the source code or classes. The fully qualified name consists of the package and the class name. Import statements are used to provide the proper location for the compiler to discover that particular class.

For instance, the following line would ask the compiler to load all the classes available in directory java_installation/java/io –

```
import java.io.*;
```

3.9. CLASSES AND OBJECTS IN PYTHON

Python is one of the most used OOP languages. This implies that almost all the code is applied through a special construct known as classes. Programmers utilize the classes in order to keep connected things together. This is done using the keyword "class." This entire process can be termed as the grouping of object-oriented constructs.

A class can be defined as the coded template that is used for creating objects. The objects in programs contain various member variables and have certain behavior and attributes that describe and represent those attributes with them. In Python programming language, a class is created by the keyword class.

On the other hand, an object is created with the help of the constructor of the class. The, the object is known as the instance of the class. In Python programming language, various instances are created by the following method:

Instance = class (arguments)

3.9.1. How to Create a Class in Python Programming Language

The simplest and the easiest class can be formed by using the class keyword. For instance, it is very easy to create a simple and empty class that contains no functionalities.

```
>>> class Reptile:
pass
>>> reptile = Reptile ()
>>> print (reptile)
<__main__.Reptile object at 0x7f315c573550>
```

3.10. ATTRIBUTES AND METHODS IN PYTHON PROGRAMMING LANGUAGE

If there is no functionality present inside the class, then a class is of no use in itself. This explains the role of functionalities in forming a class. It has been observed that functionalities are defined by setting attributes. Attributes usually act as the containers for data and functions that are connected to those particular attributes. These types of functions are known as methods.

3.10.1. Attributes in Python Programming Language

In simple words, attributes refer to the characteristics of any object. In Python programming language, attributes refer to the containers of the data and functions that are associated to the particular attributes. In the example given below, the following class can be named with the name Reptile. There will be an attribute name given to this class.

```
>>> class Reptile:
... name = "snake" # set an attribute 'name' of the class
```

It is very easy to assign the class to any variable. The process of assigning the class to any variable is known as the object instantiation. Once the class has been assigned to the variable, it is then easy to access the attributes that are present inside that particular class with the help of the dot ." operator.

For example, in the example mentioned above with class name Reptile, it is easy to access the attribute name of the class Reptile.

```
>>> # instantiate the class Reptile and assign it to variable reptile
>>> reptile = Reptile()
>>> # access the class attribute name inside the class Reptile.
>>> print(reptile.name)
snake
```

3.10.2. Methods in Python Programming Language

As soon as there are attributes present that "belong" to the class, it is easy to define functions that are capable of accessing the class attribute. These functions, that are capable of accessing the attributes, are known as methods. When the methods are defined, there is necessity to always provide the first argument to the method with a self-keyword.

For instance, let's take the example of a class Reptile. The class Reptile has a singular attribute name and one method defined by 'change_name.' The method, represented by 'change_name,' will take in an argument, known as the new_name. This argument new_name will be taken with the self-keyword.

```
>>> class Reptile:
...name = "snake"
...def change_name (self, new_name): # note that the first argument is self
...self.name = new_name # access the class attribute with the self-keyword
```

At this instance, the class Reptile can be instantiated with a variable reptile and then change the name by using the method change_name

```
>>> # instantiate the class
>>> reptile = Reptile()
>>> # print the current object name
>>> print (reptile.name)
snake
>>> # change the name using the change_name method
>>> reptile.change_name ("lizard")
>>> print(reptile.name)
lizard
```

3.10.3. Instance Attributes in Python Programming Language and the 'Init' Method

There is another method by which the values can be provided for the attributes at runtime. This process is known as init method. According to this method, the attributes are defined inside the init method. The example given below will represent the init method.

```
class Reptile:
def __init__(self, name):
self.name = name
def change_name(self, new_name):
self.name = new_name
```

After using the above statements, it is possible to directly define different attribute values for different objects. For example:

```
>>> # two variables are instantiated
>>> snake = Reptile("snake")
>>> lizard = Reptile("lizard")
>>> # print the names of the two variables
>>> print(snake.name)
snake
>>> print(lizard.name)
lizard
```

3.11. CONCLUSION

Classes and objects are some of the most important aspects of the programs written in the various OOP languages. Some of the frequently used programming languages in the modern times are C++, Java, and Python. Although the concept of classes and objects is same for every programming language, the syntax for declaring classes and objects is completely different in each programming language. Every programmer must have the basic understanding of the classes and objects. The basic concept of classes and objects makes it easy to write the program in any of the programming language.

REFERENCES

1. Bhattacharjee, J., (2020). *Classes And Objects I Tutorials & Notes | Python | Hackerearth.* [online] HackerEarth. Available at: https://www.hackerearth.com/practice/python/object-oriented-programming/classes-and-objects-i/tutorial/ (accessed on 4 June 2020).
2. Kariya, A., (2020). *C++ Classes and Objects-Geeksforgeeks.* [online] GeeksforGeeks. Available at: https://www.geeksforgeeks.org/c-classes-and-objects/ (accessed on 4 June 2020).
3. Miglani, G., (2020). *Classes and Objects in Java-Geeksforgeeks.* [online] GeeksforGeeks. Available at: https://www.geeksforgeeks.org/classes-objects-java/ (accessed on 4 June 2020).
4. Ncl.ucar.edu. (2020). *Understanding Classes and Objects.* [online] Available at: https://www.ncl.ucar.edu/Document/HLUs/User_Guide/classes/classoview.shtml (accessed on 4 June 2020).
5. Tutorialspoint.com. (2020). *Java-Object and Classes-Tutorialspoint.* [online] Available at: https://www.tutorialspoint.com/java/java_object_classes.htm (accessed on 4 June 2020).
6. W3schools.com. (2020). *Java Classes and Objects.* [online] Available at: https://www.w3schools.com/java/java_classes.asp (accessed on 4 June 2020).
7. www.javatpoint.com. (2020). *Difference between Object and Class-Javatpoint.* [online] Available at: https://www.javatpoint.com/difference-between-object-and-class (accessed on 4 June 2020).
8. Yaiser, M., (2011). *Object-Oriented Programming Concepts: Objects and Classes | Adobe Developer Connection.* [online] Adobe.com. Available at: https://www.adobe.com/devnet/actionscript/learning/oop-concepts/objects-and-classes.html (accessed on 4 June 2020).
9. Zandbergen, P., (2020). *Object-Oriented Programming: Objects, Classes and Methods.* [online] Study.com. Available at: https://study.com/academy/lesson/oop-object-oriented-programming-objects-classes-interfaces.html (accessed on 4 June 2020).

CHAPTER

4

CONTROL SYSTEM, ARRAYS, AND FUNCTIONS

CONTENTS

The chapter of the control system, arrays, and functions explains the basic significance and basic fundamentals of the computer control systems. This chapter also provides highlights on the characteristics of the computer control system such as fast calculation speed, several numbers of various forms of input and output devices, high capacity data storage, programmable control, possible telecommunications, small, and light design.

This chapter explains the important components of a computer control system such as a microprocessor, the interface of the computer control system. This chapter also mentions benefits, the working of the computer control system, along with the example on the application of computer control automation. This chapter also addresses several numbers of various control systems such as linear control system, non-linear control system, analog or continuous system, digital or discrete system, single-input single-output (SISO) systems, multi-input multi-output (MIMO) systems, lumped parameter system, and distributed parameter system.

This chapter also provides highlights on the control system modeling and simulation such as modeling purpose and simulation accuracy, modeling synchronization and node tasking, and system development and tool implementation. This chapter also explains the basic significance of an array, several numbers of various kinds of arrays such as a single-dimensional array, two-dimensional array, multidimensional, or the three-dimensional array. This chapter also mentions the character array of the string, types of indexing in the array, and the advantages of using the arrays.

4.1. INTRODUCTION TO COMPUTER CONTROL SYSTEMS

In the present interval of time, talking about the modern cities, several numbers of facilities as well as works are regulated with the help of computer systems and automation systems. For instance, Matt's trace route (MTR), electricity supply system, traffic light control system, elevators, and computerized numerical control (CNC) machines in factories.

There are several numbers of advantages of the application of the automation system, like the increment in the effectiveness, decrement in the cost, the numbers of operators, repetitive as well as boring work, improving the safety of the workers, enhancement in the working performance and completing the work that cannot be done without the use of automation (Figure 4.1).

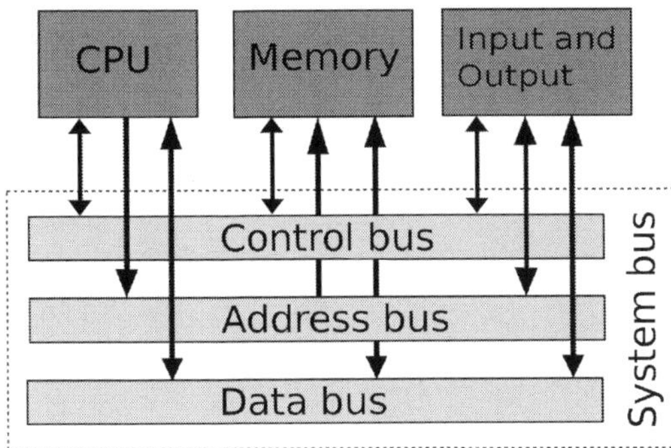

Figure 4.1. An illustration of computer control system.

Source: Image by Wikipedia.

Computer is not the only method in order to regulate the automation system. There are several numbers of other methods that are consisting of mechanical systems, electrical (or relay) systems, pneumatic system, electronic system, etc.

Yet the control system has several numbers of various advantages over the other control systems. For instance, it has fast calculation speed, multiple types of inputs and output devices, large memory, programmable control, telecommunication possible, small, and light, and so on.

4.1.1. Fast Calculation Speed

The central processing unit (CPU) of the modern or advanced computers can perform huge amount of calculations within the time period of one second, and also, it can organize huge amount of work as well as huge amount of data in a short interval of time (Figure 4.2).

Figure 4.2. Fast calculation speed.

Source: Image by public domain pictures.

The fast calculations speeds of the computer make it possible in order to regulate several numbers of things at same time under the various settings. For example, the MTR computer system can regulate or manage trains in several numbers of various routes in order to make sure that the system runs normally.

4.1.2. Multiple Forms of Input and Output Devices

Computer has several numbers of various methods in which the input command can be given, for example, keyboard, mouse, scanner, taps, and so on. In addition to this, it can also use electronic circuits in order to transform signals from the electronic sensors to the digital data and the input them to the computers.

For instance, with the help of a sensor, the temperature can be transformed into the digital data and input in the computer (Figure 4.3).

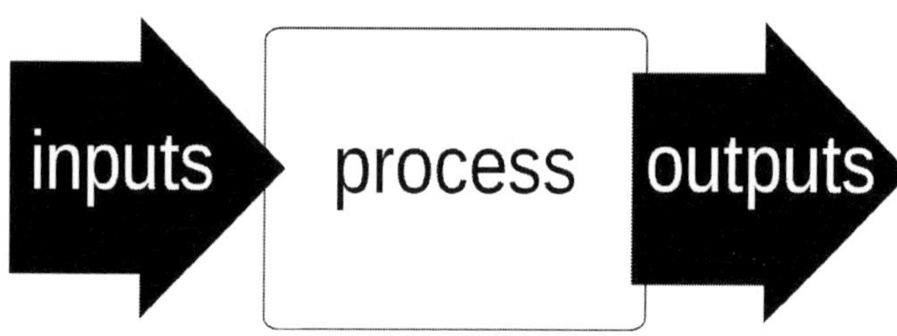

Figure 4.3. Input output system.

Source: Image by Wikimedia commons.

After the processing of the data, the computer can develop or create the output signals. In the same way, computers can also use electronic circuits in order to output the digital signals which can then be regulate several numbers of various output devices. For instance, printer, monitor, relay, motor, electromagnetic detecting valve, and so on.

4.1.3. High Capacity of Data Storage

Computers can utilize a huge number of information or data storage devices, for example, floppy disk, magnetic tape, hard disk, compact disc-read-only memory (CD-ROM), DVD, and so on. In this way, computer can use that stored data or stored information in order to perform the controlling work.

For instance, if any individual uses computer in order to design a complex shape of work piece. Then he or she input the related or appropriate data or appropriate information into the storage devices of the CNC machine and let the computer manage the cutting work of the work piece as per the data fed into the system.

4.1.4. Programmable Control

A program is a group of commands or instructions. The system of the computer can operate as per the instructions and commands of the program. In this way, operators can either input new program or alter the existing program in order to change the working procedure or methods as per the requirements.

In this way, the computer control system not only can operate those simple task and repetitive work, but in addition to this, it can also operate complex work under the various settings as well as feedback according as the commands or the instructions of the program.

4.1.5. Possible Telecommunications

Computers can be used in order to input digital signals and output the digital signals, and with the help of wires in order to transmit the signals, exchange information and communicate. In this way, computer information can be conveyed to the distant areas with the help of private cables, telephone lines, internet or radio waves.

For instance, with the help of computers, distant video cameras as well as machines can be regulated with the help of the internet. In addition to this, computers can also be used in order to control spacecrafts in space with the help of radio waves.

4.1.6. Small and Light

The size of the computers as well as the weight of the computers have been reduced, and it is all possible just because of the advancements in the technology. In the recent interval of time, the development of the microcomputers, that are so sophisticated due to the which it is possible to put the microcomputers into a number of utensils, like washing machines, refrigerators, air conditions, cars, and so on.

Taking the example of a car, in the context of those, who are using cars, they have conventional emulsifier engine, the amount of the supply of the petrol to the engine is regulated with the help of emulsifier. But, in the present interval of time, some of the cars has an Electronic Fuel Injection

(EFI) system. The work of an Electronic Fuel Injection system is that, it decides the best possible or optimal amount of supply of petrol to the engine depending to the amount of input of the air, temperature of the air, spinning speed of the engine, the temperature of the coolant, open width of valve, the concentration of the oxygen in the air vent pipe as well as the other vital aspects.

4.2. COMPUTER CONTROL SYSTEM

A control system regulates, give commands, conduct or manages the behavior of the other devices or the systems with the help of control loops. It can range from a single home heating controller with the help of thermostat controlling a domestic boiler to a large industrial control system which are used in order to regulate the processes or regulates the machine.

A control loop is the basic or an important building block of the industrial control systems. It is consisting of all the physical elements and control functions necessary in order to regulate or alter the value of a measured process variable (PV) to the value which is equal to the required set point (SP).

It is consisting of the process sensor, the controller function, and the final control element (FCE) which all are necessary for the automatic control.

A control system is a type of the computer system that regulates, gives commands and conduct the other devices or the other systems. They are open control systems as well as closed loop systems. They generally take an input, process it and get an output.

4.2.1. Microprocessor

Talking about the microprocessor, it is a tiny integrated circuit. The microprocessor has the ability to process huge amount of data very quickly. A microprocessor not only can be used as a CPU of the computer, but also, a microprocessor can also be functions as other utensil in order to increase its usage (Figure 4.4).

Figure 4.4. An illustration of microprocessor.

Source: Image by wallpaper flare.

For instance, SIM card, computer sewing machine, computer aided design (CAD) system, and so on. In this way, the use or the application of the microprocessor is very broad.

4.2.2. The Working of the Computer Control System

In the context to the computer control system, the sensors are being used in order to gather the data or information and then it is fed into the computer system. There are several numbers of various types of sensors that are being used to do so. For instance, thermal sensors, light sensors, proximity sensors, and so on.

Sensors have the ability to produce electrical signals according to the external change. For instance, resistors that are light sensitive, can be used as a light sensor. And the reason behind this is the resistance and respective current will change according to the intensity of the light that is present in the environment.

The computer processes the input signals. The signals then transmit the output signals to the components which are working or connected under the control of that signal. For example, light emitting diode (LED), relay, and so on, in order to respond respectively.

For instance, in an automatic street lightning system, when the computer sense that the light is dim, it will send instructions or the commands to the relay. The rely will then turn on the street lamps which uses a large current.

Never the less, any sort of input and output signals of the computer requires interface and supplementary equipment. In the context of computer system, the data collector will firstly gather the data or the information with the help of the sensors, and then it transforms them into the form of digital signals.

After then, it will input the data into the computer system with the help of the input interface. Keyboard and monitor can be used in order to input the control value, read the latest processed data and the input command, and so on.

The proposed signals will then output to the relay, digital or analog converter, LED along with the other execution components with the help of the output interface. The CPU will then give the command to the other parts in order to finish the desired work of the program.

With respect to the closed loop control system, the output signals will be sent back to the data collector as "feedback," and the timing machine in the computer will decide the speed of the entire loop.

4.2.3. Interface

In the context of the communication devices, each, and every communication device is consisting of an interface. The interface is in the form of a hardware or a software as well. With respect to the computer control system, the interface corresponds to the connection between the computer and all other input devices. It can also connect the computer to the other electronic systems.

The input interface is responsible in order to store and process the signals that are being transmitted from the data collector temporarily. Then it will transfer the data to the microprocessor in order to process and evaluate it.

The work of an output interface is to store the signals that are being transmitted from the microprocessor temporarily, and the signals will then be processed in order to become some controlling commands for other parts as well.

In order to elevate the output power, the output signals of the computer can be used in order to conduct the electrical, mechanical, as well as pneumatic systems with the help of several numbers of various interface. Talking about the pneumatic system, never the less, some control systems are consisting of only pneumatic components, but also, the cost will be higher.

If the pneumatic system is being used in the computer in order to regulate and install some electro-pneumatic components in the system, the cost will be much cheaper as compared to the solely pneumatic components. In the present interval of time, several numbers of various control valves can work at low voltage.

4.2.4. Example on the Application of Computer Control Automation

In this instance, the computer programs will regulate the Light Emitting Diodes (LEDs) to the light at the right time, and arrange them in order to produce various pictures, words or symbols, in order to show the regular updated information.

4.3. THE RESTRICTIONS OF COMPUTER CONTROL SYSTEM

There are several numbers of various advantages of the computer system, but on the other hand of the play, there are some restrictions as well. For instance, the cost of the computer control system is very high.

It is quite a challenging task in order to maintain the computer control system, and the control is complexed as well.

It is a hard task in order to withstand adverse environment and it required a huge number of accessory devices (Figure 4.5).

4.3.1. High Cost

In order to design and make a computer control system, it will take a long interval of time. The equipment is very costly in nature, and in this way, the total cost is high.

For instance, when a computer is used in order to regulate a cutting machine, an appropriate set of control program or instructions are required in order to control the moving path of the tools, the moving speed of the tool, rate of spin, feeding rate, change of tools, adding of coolants, and so on.

Figure 4.5. Computer control systems are expensive in nature.

Source: Image by pxhere.

4.3.2. Difficulties in Maintenance

In the present interval of time, computers are used in order to generate mass production of integrated circuits and the electronic circuit board. Computers require new parts or components in order to replace them with the damaged parts.

With the rapid development in the technology of the computer, the newly designed parts may not be used in those old-fashioned electronic circuit boards, and in this way, the maintenance of the computer control systems are very challenging task.

For instance, when a newly designed Random-Access Memory (RAM) is produced, the production of the old designed Random-Access Memory will cease. After some interval of time, when the old designed Random-Access Memory is damaged, it cannot be replaced.

4.3.3. Intolerance Under Adverse Environment

The electronic components of the computer system cannot work under the condition of bad environment. for instance, too hot, too cold, humid, dusty, vigorous vibration, and so on. In this way, it should be better to avoid the application or use of the computer control system under these sorts of settings. For instance, it is recommended to avoid the use of the cooling fan in order to cooldown the computer which is placed in a dusty location.

4.3.4. Requirement of Large Amount of Supporting Device

Computers can regulate or manage the large amount of data in a short interval of time, but it requires some sort of supporting devices in order to provide the information. What is why a computer control system requires several numbers of various supporting devices.

For instance, a system is required in order to identify the location of the tools and the location of the work piece when a computer is used in order to control a cutting machine. The system can give feedback to the computers in order to permit it to regulate the machine correspondingly.

4.4. TYPES OF CONTROL SYSTEMS

A computer control system is a system of devices that regulates, commands, conducts or manages the behavior of the other devices in order to accomplish the required outcome. In simple words, the definition of a control system can be explained as a system that controls the other systems in order to accomplish the required state.

There are several numbers of different types of control systems, which can be broadly considered as a linear control systems or non-linear control systems. These sorts of control systems are explained in the detail below.

4.4.1. Linear Control Systems

To understand the linear control system, first of all it requires to understand the basic fundamental of the superposition. The basic fundamental of the superposition theorem is consisting of the two important qualities and they are mentioned below:

Homogeneity: A system is known to be homogeneous in nature, when multiplying the inputs with some constant "A," then the output will also be multiplied by the same value of constant (that is A).

Additivity: Let's assume, there is a system S and giving the input to this system as a1 for the first time and as an outcome, the output which is getting is as b1 with respect to the input a1. On the second time, when giving input a2 and with respect to this, the outcome will be the output as b2.

Now, let's suppose this time giving input as a summation of the previous inputs (that is a1 plus a2) and with respect to this input, let's assume, the output will be (b1 plus b2). In this way, it could be said that system S is following the property of additivity. Now, it is quite easy in order to determine the linear control systems as those types of control systems which follow the principle of homogeneity as well as additivity.

Examples of Linear Control System: Let's assume a solely resistive network which is having a constant direct current (DC) source. This circuit follows the principle of the homogeneity as well as the principle of additivity. All the undesired impacts are avoided and supposing the ideal behavior of each and every element which is present in the network, it could be said that, as an outcome, will get linear voltage and the current properties.

This is an example of the linear control system.

4.4.2. Non-linear Control Systems

The definition of the non-linear control system is that, a control system which does not obey the principles or fundamentals of the homogeneity. With respect to the real life, all of the control systems that are non-linear systems (linear control systems only exist in theory). The explaining function is an approximate procedure in order to analyze the certain sort of non-linear control issues.

Examples of Non-linear System: Talking about the example of a non-linear system, a well-known instance of a non-linear system is a magnetization curve or no-load curve of a DC machine. It will be discussed briefly about the no-load cure of DC machines here. No load curve provides the connection among the air gap flux and the field winding mmf.

It is crystal clear that there is a linear connection among the winding mmf and the air gap flux but after this, saturation has come which depicts the non-linear behavior of the curve or the properties of the non-linear control system.

4.4.3. Analog or Continuous System

With respect to these sorts of control systems, that is analog or a continuous system, there is a continuous signal in the form of input to the system. These sorts of signals are the continuous function of the time. There could be several numbers of different source of continuous input signals such as sinusoidal type signal input source, square type of the signal input source. The signal can be in the form of the continuous triangle and so on.

4.4.4. Digital or Discrete System

In these sorts of control system, which is digital system or discrete system, there is a discrete signal 9 or signal may be in the form of the pulse) as the input to the system. These sorts of signals have a discrete interval of time.

The several numbers of various sources of continuous sources can be converted, such as sinusoidal type signal input source, square type of the signal input source and so on, into a discrete form with the help of a switch.

Now, there are several numbers of different advantages of discrete system or digital system over the analog system and these advantages are mentioned as follows:

1 Digital systems or discrete systems can manage the non-linear control system more efficiently when it is compared with the analog type of control systems;
2. With respect to digital systems or discrete systems, the requirement of the power is much less when it is compared with the analog control systems;
3. Digital systems or discrete systems has a higher rate of precision and they can be very useful in performing several numbers of various complicated computations very easily when it is compared with the analog systems;
4. With respect to the reliability, digital systems or discrete systems are more reliable when they are compared with the analog systems. Digital systems or discrete systems also have a small and compact size;
5. Digital systems or discrete systems works on the logical operation, which elevates their precision many folds; and
6. With respect to the digital systems or discrete systems, losses are less when they are compared with the analog systems in general.

4.4.5. Single Input Single Output Systems

These sorts of control systems are also known as SISO types of system. In case of SISO (which is short form of single output single input systems), the system has a single input for a single output. There are several numbers of different example of this type of system, such as temperature control system, position control system, and so on.

4.4.6. Multiple Input Multiple Output Systems

These types of control systems are also known as MIMO type of system. In the case of MIMO (which is the short form of multi input multi output system), the system has several numbers of multiple outputs with respect to the multiple inputs. There are several numbers of different example of this type of control system, such as PLC type system, and so on.

4.4.7. Lumped Parameter System

In the case of these sorts of control system, the several numbers of different active as well as passive components are supposed to be concentrated at a point, and this is the reason, that they are known as lumped parameter type of system. Analysis of these sort of systems are very easy which can be consisting of differential equations.

4.4.8. Distributed Parameter System

With respect to these sorts of control system, that is distributed parameter control system, the several numbers of different active (such as inductors and capacitors) as well as passive parameters (such as resistors) are supposed to be distributed uniformly length-wise. That is the main reason that, these sorts of control systems are known as distributed parameter type of system.

Analysis of these sorts of system is quite challenging which is consisting of partial differential equations (PDEs).

4.5. HOW DOES A CONTROL SYSTEM WORK?

In order to understand that how a control system works, it provides assistance in order to remember how a computer system is structured.

1. The input devices, generally sensors, send data readings to the microprocessor (or the computer) at set interval of time;
2. In order to be acknowledged, this data may have to be transformed with the help of an ADC (which is analog to the digital converter);
3. The microprocessor compares the readings of the data against the pre-set values that it has stored (with the help of a control program);
4. The microprocessor then makes a decision as to whether any action is required (for example, is more heat is required in order to maintain the pre-set value?);

5. If it is required, the microprocessor will send a signal in order to instruct an output device to do something (for example turn on heater, turn off oxygen pump, and so on);
6. This can be consisting of an actuator (for example a motor, in order to open the gates or shop doors); and
7. This process repeats in a continuous loop.

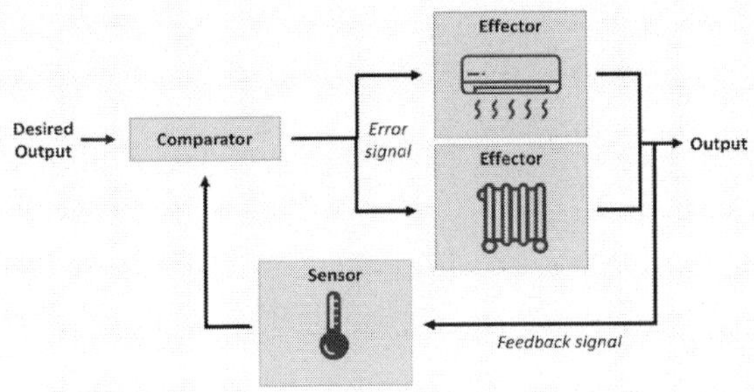

Figure 4.6. Working of a closed loop or a feedback control system.

Source: Image by Wikimedia commons.

4.5.1. Benefits of Control Systems

1. Computers control systems are very fast in order to respond to change or alter and can process the data very quickly;
2. Computer control system can run all every day, every second, without wages or needing a break;
3. Computer control system can operate in places dangerous with respect to the humans; and
4. Computer control systems are very consistent and precise with zero error.

4.6. EXAMPLES OF COMPUTER CONTROL SYSTEM

4.6.1. Traffic Light

Talking about the simple traffic light, in the traffic light the input is a timer, which decides what lights are needed to be turned on. More complex versions, every so often are consisting of sensors that detects the presence of metal on the cars which are moving on the streets (Figure 4.7).

Figure 4.7. An illustration of traffic light.

Source: Image from pexels.

This permits for more dynamic timing, so that for example, pedestrians do not have to wait when there are no cars present on the streets or roads. In addition to this, another use of these sort of sensors are to regulate the traffic lights for the emergency situations, for example, in order to turn on the green signal when fire truck is approaching.

4.6.2. GPS (Global Positioning System)

The Global Positioning System (GPS) is basically a navigation system which is based on the satellites. The GPS is made up of network of a sum of twenty-four satellites that are moving in the Earth's orbit.

Figure 4.8. An illustration of global positioning system.

Source: Image by pixabay.

The location of a user is identified with the help of measuring the distance to three or four satellites, taking the point of intersection in a process, which is known as trilateration. In order for this to work, each, and every satellite carries an atomic clock, in such a way that the distance between the receiver of the GPS and the GPS satellite can be evaluated with the help of an exact time differences.

4.6.3. Automatic Doors

Automatic doors are consisting of a sensor, in which the sensors are continuously checks if a person is in front of the door. If there is any kind of presence, an actuator, which in this case usually a motor, open the doors. The sensors can be based on the motions or they can be based on the pressure.

4.6.4. Heating Systems

The control systems compare the actual state (for example, the temperature) with the target state and then it takes the actions which are required. The control system is also programmable and can be consisting of the time schedules, set points (SPs), controllers, logic, timers, alarms, trend logs, and so on.

4.6.5. Taxi Meter

A taxi meter evaluates the count of the passenger fare in the taxis that are usually based on the waiting time and the distance which has been traveled (Figure 4.9).

Figure 4.9. An illustration of a taxi meter.

Source: Image by flickr.

4.6.6. Elevator

The control system in an elevator takes inputs from the several numbers of different keys (direction, hold door, door open, door close, floor, and so on), and the position sensors and gives the various outputs according to that particular input.

Outputs are the display of the current floor, direction of the lift in which it is moving (upwards or downwards) and control of the door and the motors that do the work of lifting the car or lift upwards or downwards.

4.6.7. Washing Machine

The microcontrollers in a washing machine just get inputs from the user (with the help of pressing the buttons or switches) about how long the wash is going to take place (as per required by the user), the temperature of washing, along with the speed. And then brings this into the action, with the help of regulating the motors, and so on. Moreover, washing machine also offers pre-defined programs for washing.

4.6.8. Process Control

A control system that is in charge of keeping the particular sort of process' output within a required range. It generally takes a different outputs foe this. Process control is used in the industry which allows mass production of consistent products such as chemicals, paper pollution, oil refining, power plants, and other as well. Process control also permits or allows the automation, which requires less staff. Control is generally based on the feedback loops.

4.6.9. Device Drivers

A device driver is an interface between the Operating system and a hardware device. Inputs or instructions are provided with the help of program. Then the work of the driver is to translate or convert the instructions for this device and gets data back. These drivers then present these data to the program.

4.6.10. Cleaning Robot

Infrared sensors can detect the objects which are placed in front of them. If the robot senses the presence of an object, then it processes these data and moves away in a different direction. It has a specific algorithm each time it receives something from the sensors.

4.7. COMPUTER CONTROL SYSTEM MODELING AND SIMULATION

Modeling and the simulation activities in the computer systems could provide advantages if the following technical issues are taken into the account.

4.7.1. Modeling Purpose and Simulation Accuracy

One well-known difficulties in the modeling is to have the potential in order to determine the accuracy which is required for the given purpose. Taking an example, the execution of a data-flow over two processors and a serial network.

A huge span of modeling detail is possible, ranging from a simple delay over the discrete event resource management models (for example, processor, and the communication scheduling) to the low-level behavioral models.

The mapping of these sorts of details between the models and the real computer networks will alter the timing behavior of the functions because of the effects, for example, delays, and jitter. Some of the reflections are connected to this are mentioned below:

1. The introduction of "application level effects," for example, delays, jitter, and data loss, into a control design, could be a suitable abstraction with respect to the control engineering. The "mapping" to the actual computer system can be nontrivial.

For instance, the reason of delays and jitter could be several numbers of different combinations of execution, communication, interference, and blocking. More accurate or more precise computer system models will be needed in order to compare the other designs or architecture, and in order to provide the approximation of the system behavior. In addition to this, modeling is a kind of prototyping, and such vital role in the process of designing.

2. It is quite fascinating that some models of the computer system could be more or less detailed, given the right abstraction. For instance, if fairly detailed Computer Area Network model has been developed, it could still be used with respect to the control system simulation given that it is appropriately effective in order to simulate and that its complicatedness is masked away.
3. It is very obvious that the several different models of the computer system are need to reflect the real system. In the early stages, the models or the architecture only exists on the "drawing board." As the design proceeds, more, and more details will be available. As an outcome, the models that are used with respect to the analysis must be updated with respect to that.

4. In order to accomplish the accuracy, a close cooperation between the software developers as well as hardware developed is importantly required and it is required at every point of stage through the course of the development of the system.

4.7.2. Global Synchronization and Node Tasking

Both synchronous system as well as asynchronous systems exist. With respect to the industries, the asynchronous systems lead but this can alter with the introduction of new as well as safety critical applications, for example, steer-by-wire in cars, and due to the advantages that are inherent in distributed systems based on a global clock.

Talking about a microscope, generally, the communication circuits are hard synchronized that is needed to have the potential in order to receive bits and arbitrate appropriately. With respect to a system which is low-level synchronized, and/or synchronized clocks, the synchronization could fail in several numbers of various ways.

With respect to the asynchronous systems, the clock drift could be of interest in order to incorporate. Given the several numbers of various clocks with various speeds, this will impact or influence all durations within each and every node.

A traditional way of expressing the duration is simply with the help of a time value. With respect to this, the values could possibly be scaled through the course of the simulation setup. All the above-mentioned behaviors could be of interest in order to model and simulate.

Undoubtedly, the most important aspect or property of a distributed computer system is its communication potential. In early stages of design, the distributed and communication characteristics are every so often targeted first; but then node scheduling also becomes interesting and is, in this way, of high relevance.

It is very common that several numbers of activities co-exist on nodes. Also, these sorts of activities generally have various timing requirements and may also be safety critical with respect to several numbers of various degrees.

The scheduling on the nodes impacts the distributed system with the help of causing local delays that can impact the behavior of the overall system.

Through the course of the development of a distributed control system, somehow the functions and the elements, which are of need to be placed to the nodes. The fundamental meaning of this is that an execution independent functional design that is required to be improved with the help of a new "system" functions, which for instance:

1. Perform communication among the various parts of the control system, now residing on various nodes;
2. Perform scheduling of the computer system processors and networks;
3. Perform additional error detection as well as handling in order to cater for new failure modes (for example, broken network, temporary node failure, and so on).

A node is made up with the help of application activities, system software which are consisting of a real-time kernel, low-level Input or Output drivers, along with the hardware functions that emphasize the communication interface.

1. The node task model needs to include the following:
   i . A definition of tasks, their triggers, and execution times for "execution units."
   ii. A definition of the interactions between tasks with respect to thc scheduling, inter task communication, as well as resource sharing.
   iii. A definition of the real-time kernel and other system software in the context of execution time, blocking, and so on. Some issues in the further development are consisting of what sorts of inter task communication and synchronization should be supported (for example, signals, mailboxes, semaphores, and so on).

In addition to this, whether, and to what degree, there is a necessity in order to well thought out the hierarchical and hybrid scheduling (for example, including both processor's interrupt as well as real-time kernel scheduling levels).

2. **The Functional Model:** The functional method is used in traditional control design should be reusable within the combined function computer models. This shows or depicts that it should be possible in order to somehow adapt or modify the functional models in order to integrate or combine a node level tasking model.
3. **Communication Models:** The kinds of communication protocols are confined with the help of the area under the consideration. None the less, at present interval of time, there are several number of various communication protocols are being developed in view

of future embedded control systems. Computer Area Network is currently a de facto standard, but there is also an interest in including the following:

Time triggered Computer Area Network referring to Computer Area Network systems which is designed or architecture in order to integrate the clock synchronization which is suitable for the distributed control applications.

This depends on the ability of the recent International Organization for Standardization (ISO) revision of Computer Area Network in order to easily implement the clock synchronization in Computer Area Network and where the retransmissions can be turned off.

Characteristics that depicts the state-of-the-art fault-tolerant protocols, for example, the Time-Triggered Protocol. Fault-tolerance mechanisms of these protocols, for example, membership management and atomic broadcast, then they are required to be suitably modeled.

4. **Fault Models:** The use of fault models plays a very important or vital role with respect to the design of dependable systems. The particular sorts of models of interest are very application specific. For inclusion in models and simulation, it is of interest in order to find out the generic fault models along with their execution.

There are several numbers of various studies are available in the context of fault models that are addressing the transient as well as permanent hardware faults, and to some degree also classifying the design faults. As always, there is also the problem of insertion as a fault, an error, or a failure. As an outcome, this is a prioritized topic for further work.

4.7.3. System Development and Tool Implementation

Through the course of the development of the distributed control systems, it would be very helpful in order to have a simulation tool box or a library in which the user can build the system that are based on the prebuilt modules in order to define the things, for example, the network protocols along with the scheduling algorithms.

With the help of this kind of tool, the user can concentrate on the application details instead. This kind of tool is possible from the time, when components such as several kinds of schedulers and Computer Area Network and standardized across application are well explained.

In the similar manner, a programmer works on a specific level of abstraction at which the hardware as well as the operating system details are hidden with the help of compiler, and the simulation tool should give the user a high level of abstraction in order to develop the application.

This sort of tool will implement a limitation between the application and the rest of the system. This will provide assistance in order to pace up the rate of development process, and provides the developers an extra flexibility with respect to the development of the application.

It is quite clear that the execution of this sort of hybrid systems that are aiming to model necessitates a deep understanding and knowledge of the application of the simulation tool. Co-simulation of the hybrid systems necessitates the simulation engine in order to control both, parts that are time driven, along with the parts that are event driven.

The former is consisting of sampled subsystems as well as the continuous time systems, that are controlled with the help of a numerical integration algorithm that can be based on a fixed or varying step size. The latter can be consisting of state machines along with the other sorts of event-triggered logic.

Some of the characteristics that are required to take into the consideration with respect to the execution of tools are mentioned as follows:

1. If events are used in the computer system model these must be identified with the help of the simulation engine. How is the event detection mechanism implemented in the simulation tool?
2. At which simulation steps are the actions of a state flow system carried out?
3. How can actions be defined to be atomic (carried out through the course of one simulation step)?
4. How can preemption of simulation be executed including temporary blocking to model the effects of computer system scheduling?

4.8. WHAT IS ARRAY?

Data structure which contains a group of elements is known as array. In general, it is said that all those elements which are in the data structure are all of the same data type, such as an integer or string. To organize data so that a related set of values can be easily sorted or searched and for this array are commonly used in computer programs (Figure 4.10).

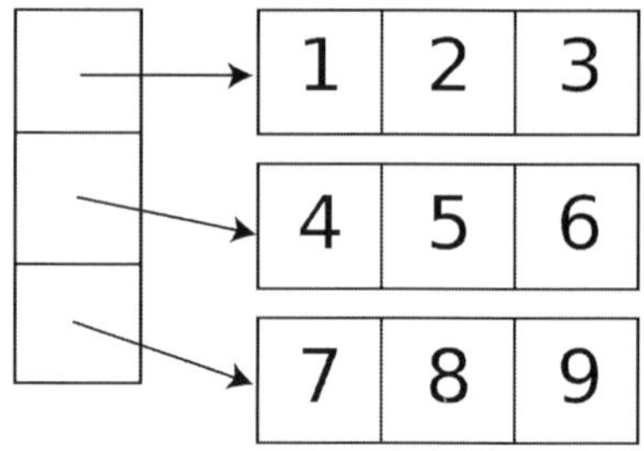

Figure 4.10. An illustration of an array.

Source: Image by Wikipedia.

For instance, web pages which are found in a search performed by the user, a search engine may use an array to store these web pages. The program will output one element of the array at a time, when the results are being displayed.

For a specified number of values or until all the values stored in the array have been output this may be done. In a way to manage memory with security storing the results in an array is much more efficient. And the storing in array is required for a specific period of time, till the program could create a new variable for each result found.

The syntax for storing and displaying the values in an array typically looks something like this:

Array name [0] = "This";

Array name [1] = "is";

Array name [2] = "pretty simple";

print array name [0];

print array name [1];

print array name [2];

The first three values of the array are printed by using the above commands, or there is another way which is very simple, as by using a "while" or "for" loop, the programmer can tell the program to output each value in the array until the last value has been reached. Therefore, it has been observed that an array is not only used for helping manage memory more efficiently, and they also help in making the programmer's job more efficient as well.

The various types of Array those are provided by c as follows:

4.8.1. Single Dimensional Array

For representing the elements of the array, a dimensional is used for example

int a[5]

The [] is used for dimensional or the sub-script of the array that is generally used for declaring the elements of the array. We can use the Subscript of the array for accessing the element from the array like this

a[3]=100

This will set the value of 4th element of array.

So, when there is only the single bracket then it called the Single Dimensional Array. This is also known as the Single Dimensional Array.

4.8.2. Two-Dimensional Array

For representing the elements of the array in the form of the rows and columns the two-dimensional arrays are used and also for representing the Matrix these are used. Two subscripts are used by the Two-dimensional array for declaring the elements of the array.

Like this int a [3][3]

So, this is the example of the two-dimensional array. In this, first [3] represents the total number of Rows and the Second [3] Represents the Total number of Columns. By Multiplying the Numbers of Rows, the Total Number of elements are judged * The Total Number of elements are 9 in the above array.

4.8.3. Multidimensional or the Three-Dimensional Array

Total Number of Tables of Matrix is represented, when there is requirement to make the two or more tables of the Matrix Elements a three-dimensional array is used for declaring the Array Elements as an individual can use the way like this

int a [3][3][3]

The total number of tables is represented in this first 3 and the second 3 represents the total number of rows in each table and the third 3 represents the total number of çç.

In this way, this means the three rows and the three columns the 3 Tables are having. The elements are stored always in the contiguous in the memory of the computer is the main and very important thing about the array.

4.8.4. Character Array of String

The Array of Characters is called the Strings. Like an integer characters are also be in the Array. For representing the Strings, everyone should always remember that a string is terminated with the \0 or Null character they are generally used.

String provided by the C Language in the String h Header are the built-in string Operation those are file like

1. Total numbers of characters in string or strlen for getting the length;
2. For concatenating the two Strings this function is used or Strconcat is used for joining the two Strings;
3. Strrev is the function which is used for obtaining the Reverse of the String; and
4. Strcmp is the function which is used for Comparing the Two Strings and it gives us the result as follows after comparing the Two Strings.

it Returns us + value

if String1 is Greater than String2

it Returns us the – Value

if String1 is Less than String2

it Returns us the 0

if string1 is Equals to String2

Like, the array elements of integer types, the character array also are the single dimensional or the two-dimensional array.

Single dimensional array-array which are used for creating the number of characters is known as the single dimensional array like

char name [10],

In this there is a way in which an individual can use the 10 characters on the name variable Means an individual can give the name as 10 characters long.

4.9. TYPES OF INDEXING IN ARRAY

1. 0 (zero-based indexing): The first element of the array is indexed by subscript of 0;
2. 1 (one-based indexing): The first element of the array is indexed by subscript of 1; and

3. n (n-based indexing): This indexing gives a facility to the base index of an array, that it can be freely chosen. Usually programming languages allowing n-based indexing also allow negative index values and other scalar data types like enumerations, or characters may be used as an array index.

4.9.1. Advantages of Using Arrays

1. Arrays allow random access of elements. This used for makes accessing elements by position faster; and
2. Arrays can make a pretty big difference in performance because it has better cache locality.

Usually, string is called an array of characters, but on the other hand an array of integers or floats is called simply an array.

4.10. CONCLUSION

The achievement or the accomplishment in the development of the software of a control system which is based on the microcomputer is very important with respect to the success of an entire system because of the reasons that are mentioned below:

1. The cost of the software plays an important role of the total system development costs;
2. The application programming language identifies the ease as well as the effectiveness of the application programming; and
3. The reliability of the software and the used self-checking features are important factors in the system availability and reliability.

The main challenging task in postulating the software for an industrial control system is to acquire a balanced solution among the system and the application software. The software should be suitably flexible in order to permit all sorts of important or vital functions that to be included. But also, in addition to this, they should be restrictive to guide the application programming.

The system developed has been used for several numbers of various application and experience has shown that the application engineers have been able to pick up the application or utilization of the new system very rapidly.

This shows that the man-machine interface among the industrial control system and the application engineers has been quite successful. The reliability record of the system has also been satisfactory, which shows that the most of the software errors have been found and eliminated as well.

REFERENCES

1. (n.d). Introduction to Computer Control Systems. [ebook] Technological Studies. Available at: https://resources.hkedcity.net/downloadResource.php?rid=576511295&pid=206501261 (accessed on 4 June 2020).
2. Björn, W. & Martin, O., (1980). Programming of Control Functions in a Microcomputer Based Control System. [online] research gate. Available at: https://www.researchgate.net/publication/333376972_PROGRAMMING_OF_CONTROL_FUNCTIONS_IN_A_MICROCOMPUTER_BASED_CONTROL_SYSTEM (accessed on 4 June 2020).
3. Christensson, P., (2017). Array Definition. [online] Techterms.com. Available at: https://techterms.com/definition/array (accessed on 4 June 2020).
4. Computer Science GCSE GURU, (2020). Control Systems-Computer Science GCSE GURU. [online] Computer Science GCSE GURU. Available at: https://www.computerscience.gcse.guru/theory/control-systems (accessed on 4 June 2020).
5. Computer science wiki, (2019). Control Systems-Computer Science Wiki. [online] Computersciencewiki.org. Available at: https://computersciencewiki.org/index.php/Control_Systems (accessed on 4 June 2020).
6. Dinesh, T., (n.d). What is Array? Type of Array. [online] ecomputernotes.com/. Available at: http://ecomputernotes.com/cpp/array-pointer-union/wh (accessed on 4 June 2020).
7. Electrical4U, (2019). Types of Control Systems | Linear and Non Linear Control System | Electrical4u. [online] Electrical4U. Available at: https://www.electrical4u.com/types-of-systems-linear-and-non-linear-system/ (accessed on 4 June 2020).
8. Geeks for Geeks, (n.d). Introduction to Arrays-Geeksforgeeks. [online] Geeks for Geeks. Available at: https://www.geeksforgeeks.org/introduction-to-arrays/ (accessed on 4 June 2020).
9. Lawrence Livermore National Laboratory, (n.d). Computer Control System. [online] Lasers.llnl.gov. Available at: https://lasers.llnl.gov/about/how-nif-works/seven-wonders/computer-control-system (accessed on 4 June 2020).
10. Science direct, (2020). Computer Control Systems: An Overview |

Sciencedirect Topics. [online] Sciencedirect.com. Available at: https://www.sciencedirect.com/topics/engineering/computer-control-systems (accessed on 4 June 2020).

11. Tutorials point, (2020). Computer Programming-Arrays-Tutorialspoint. [online] Tutorialspoint.com. Available at: https://www.tutorialspoint.com/computer_programming/computer_programming_arrays.htm (accessed on 4 June 2020).

CHAPTER

5

COMPUTING WITH MATRICES AND VECTORS

CONTENTS

Matrices and vectors are an essential part of computer programming based on numerical methods. Numerical methods and numerical analysis have been the base of so many computer programming languages. Initially, here the vectors and matrices that are used in computer programming are described. The concept of advanced matrix and blocks have also been elaborated here. The concept of qubits that are related to quantum computing is described here by taking examples of matrices and vectors used in it. Since, matrices and vectors are important part of computing, hence, it is used in quantum computing too which has been described in this chapter.

This chapter also provides information related to the allocation of vectors, matrices, and blocks. In the end, the concepts related to qubit have been discussed in an efficient manner so that it can help understand the vector concepts better.

5.1. INTRODUCTION

Matrices and vectors are the essential part of computing for numerical analysis. In this chapter, the different types, their processing rules and views have been elaborated along with their allocation and representation.

The vector and matrix concepts are significant in numerous areas of computing. The Mat lab represents MATrix LABoratory, proposing that Mat lab is structured particularly for matrices.

In physics a vector is signified with a bolt, as . In software engineering one may think about a vector as a method for information storage (like in a table), and it is frequently called array.

Vectors can be characterized as line vectors or section vectors. In computer programming one can characterize these vectors with the orders: v = [1; 3] and u = [1; 3]. Matrices and vectors are surrounded by sections, and semicolon inside the sections separate the lines.

In case of a vector there are more than one element available in the series. It could be a 1-D array, one-column matrix, one-row matrix. The length and width of the matrix are declared based on the elements present in the vector.

In instances it becomes essential to differentiate amongst exclusive types of signals that are scalar or different types of signals that are vector, the distinctions should be explicitly mentioned. For instance, the terms one-dimensional array, column vector, and row vector distinguish amongst three kinds of vector.

The size of a matrix is the pair of numbers that imply how many rows and columns the matrix has. The orientation of a 2-D vector is considered by either a row vector or a column vector. A one-dimensional array has no orientation this is in some cases called a disoriented vector.

5.2. PROCESSING RULES

The associated guidelines show how the blocks present in the Communications Toolbox process signals of scalar, vector, and matrices.

In the numerical calculations, some blocks are not recognized among one-dimensional scalars and individual frameworks.

In the event that the block delivers a scalar vector from a scalar data, the block performs dimensional shift.

For vector input signals:

- In case of most blocks the multichannel functionality is not supported and the processing of row vector is also not allowed;
- Orientation and dimension are preserved with the help of block output; and
- The difference between one-dimensional arrays and m1 matrices is not done by numerical computations.

The block considers components of the information vector as a variable that emerges normally from the block's activity or as progressive example from a solitary time arrangement.

Most blocks don't process network flags that have more than one line and more than one section. For blocks that do, a sign looking like a N/M matrix represents to a progression of N progressive examples from M channels.

An Input parameter on the block decides whether every component or a segment of the information signal, is a channel.

A few blocks, for example, the advanced baseband balance blocks, can create numerous values for each approximation of a scalar signal.

An alternative parameter on the block decides whether the extra examples are by expanding the signal production or by expanding the size of the signal. Blocks that process constant time signals don't process outline-based information sources. Such blocks incorporate the analog phase-locked loop blocks.

5.3. VECTORS AND MATRICES

The functions portrayed here give a basic vector and matrix interface to normal C clusters. The management of memory of these exhibits is represented with the help of a solitary basic type, known as a block.

By composing the functions such as vectors and networks can pass a solitary structure containing the two information and measurements without requiring extra function parameters. The structures are perfect with the vector and matrix groups used by BLAS schedules (Figure 5.1).

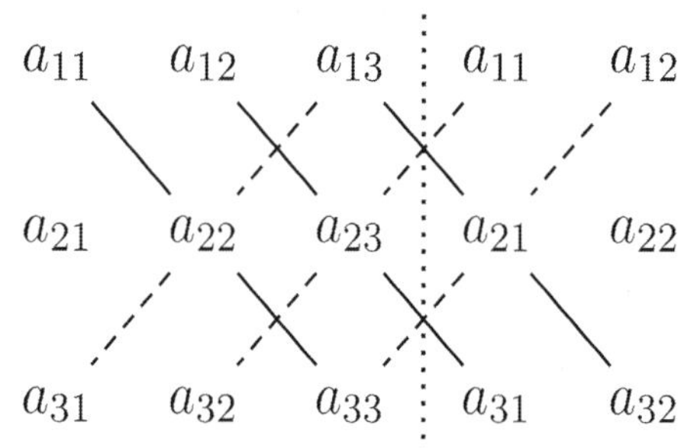

Figure 5.1. Matrices in computing.

Source: Image by Wikimedia

The most widely recognized approach to duplicate two vectors together is through the internal part. The inward part gives the projection of one vector onto another and is priceless in depicting how to communicate one vector as a whole of other more forward vectors.

It is given here that a short presentation is required to examine a standard reference on straight polynomial math, for example, Strang, G. (1993).

5.3.1. Data Types

In case of the standard data types all the functions are made available for use. The prefix gsl_block, gsl_vector, and gsl_matrix is for the versions for double-precision. Similarly, the prefix gsl_block_float, gsl_vector_float, and gsl_matrix_float is for the versions for single-precision float arrays.

5.4. ADVANCED MATRIX CONCEPTS

Let us now talk about the control of Matrices to Eigenvalues, Eigenvectors, and Exponentials which structure a key arrangement of devices that have to be described and to execute quantum calculations.

5.4.1. Eigenvalues and Eigenvectors

Suppose M is a square matrix and v be a vector that is not the zero vector. Let v be an eigen vector of M if Mv=cv for some number c. Let c is the eigen value for the eigen vector v.

Generally, a matrix M may change a vector into some other vector, however, an eigen vector is uncommon for which it is left unaltered with the exception of being duplicated by a number. Note that If v is an eigenvector with eigenvalue c, at that point av is also an eigenvector (for any nonzero a) with a similar eigenvalue.

For instance, for the identity matrix, each vector v is an eigen vector with eigen value 1. The eigen vectors of the matrix are with eigen values d1, d2, and d3, individually. If d1, d2, and d3 are particular numbers, in that case these vectors (and their products) are the main eigen vectors of the matrix D.

As a rule, for an inclining matrix it is anything but difficult to examine the eigen values and eigen vectors. The eigen values are largely the numbers showing up on the diagonal places, and their individual eigenvectors are the unit vectors with one section equivalent to 1 and the rest of the passages equivalent to 0.

Note in the above model that the eigenvectors of D structure for 3-dimensional vectors. A cluster of different vectors with the end goal that any vector can be composed as a direct combination of them. Generally, v^1, v^2 and v^3 structure a premise if any vector v can be composed as $v=a^1v^1+a^2v^2+a^3v^3$ for certain numbers a^1, a^2 and a^3.

Review that a Hermitian matrix (additionally called self-adjoint) is a square matrix that is complex and equivalent to its own intricate conjugate, while a unitary matrix is a square matrix that is complex and whose converse is equivalent to its unpredictable conjugate.

For Hermitian and unitary matrices, which are basically the main frameworks experienced in quantum processing, there is a general outcome known as the spectral theorem, which declares the accompanying: For any Hermitian or unitary matrix M, there exists a unitary U with the end goal that M=U+DU for some diagonal matrix D. Besides, the diagonal passages of D will be the eigenvalues of M.

5.4.2. Matrix Exponentials

A matrix exponential can be characterized in exact analogy to the exponential function. This is significant as per the fact that quantum mechanical time development is portrayed by a unitary matrix of the structure e^{iB} for Hermitian matrix B.

Thus, performing matrix exponentials is a key piece of quantum process and as such Q# offers characteristic schedules for describing these activities. There are numerous ways to process a matrix exponential on a computer, and in general numerically approximating such an exponential is dangerous.

The most essential approach to see how to register the exponential of a matrix is through the eigenvalues and eigenvectors of that matrix.

In particular, the spectral theorem examined above says that for each Hermitian or unitary matrix A there exists a unitary matrix U and a diagonal matrix D with the end goal that A=U+DU. In view of the properties of unitarity one should have that $A^2=U+D^2U$ and comparably for any force p Ap=U+DpU.

In other words, if the change is performed to the eigen basis of the matrix An, at that point processing the matrix exponential is comparable to processing the common exponential of the eigenvalues of the matrix.

The same number of tasks in quantum processing include performing matrix exponentials, this work of changing into the eigen basis of a matrix to simplify performing the administrator exponential shows up as often as possible and is the premise behind numerous quantum calculations, for example, Trotter-Suzuki-style quantum recreation techniques.

5.5. BLOCKS

For consistency, all memory is allocated using a gsl_block structure. The structure contains two segments, the size of memory and a pointer to the memory. The gsl_block structure resembles this, gsl_block.

Vectors and matrices are made by cutting a hidden block. A cut is a lot of components framed from an underlying balance and a mix of lists. On account of a matrix the progression size for the section list represents the column length. The progression size for a vector is known as the step. The functions for designating and deallocating blocks are characterized in gsl_block.h.

5.5.1. Block Allocation

The functions for providing memory to a block follow the style of malloc. Likewise, they additionally play out their own error checking. If there is inadequate memory accessible to assign a block, at that point the functions call the GSL error handler (with an error number of GSL_ENOMEM) notwithstanding restoring an invalid pointer.

In this manner, in the event that one utilizes the library error handler to prematurely end the program, at that point it isn't important to check each alloc. gsl_block * gsl_block_alloc (size_t n) This function distributes memory for a block of n double accuracy components, restoring a pointer to the block struct.

The block is not instated; thus, the estimations of its components are indistinct. Utilize the function gsl_block_calloc () in the event that it is needed to guarantee that all the components are introduced to zero.

Zero-sized solicitations are substantial and return a non-invalid outcome. An invalid pointer is returned if inadequate memory is accessible to make the block. gsl_block * gsl_block_calloc (size_t n).

This function assigns memory for a block and instates all the components of the block to zero. void gsl_block_free (gsl_block * b) This function liberates the memory utilized by a block b recently distributed with gsl_ block_alloc() or gsl_block_calloc().

5.5.2. Reading and Writing Blocks

The library gives functions to perusing and composing blocks to a record as double information or arranged content. int gsl_block_fwrite (FILE * stream, const gsl_block * b) This function composes the components of the block b to the stream in paired configuration.

The arrival esteem is 0 for progress and GSL_EFAILED if there was an issue making contact with the document. Since the information is written in the local parallel arrangement it may not be compact between various models.

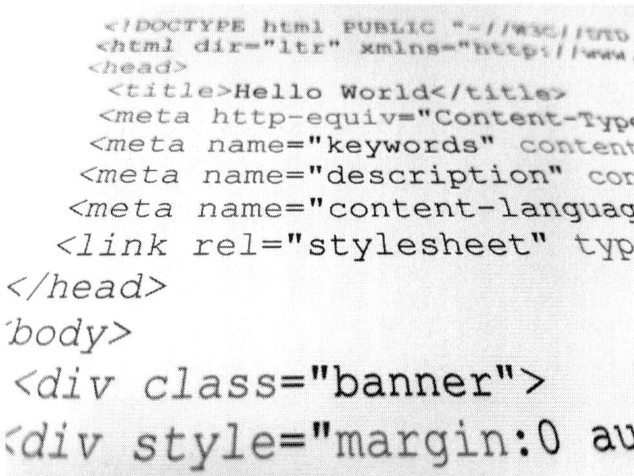

Figure 5.2. Reading and writing blocks in computer programming.

Source: Image by pxfuel.

int gsl_block_fread (FILE * stream, gsl_block * b), this function adds extra memory to the block b from the open stream in parallel arrangement. The block b must be reallocated with the right length since the function utilizes the size of b to decide what number of bytes to examine.

The arrival esteem is 0 for progress and GSL_EFAILED if there was an issue inside the document. The information is accepted to have been written in the local double arrangement on a similar design. int gsl_block_fprintf (FILE * stream, const gsl_block * b, const singe * position).

This function composes the components of the block b line-by-line to the stream utilizing the organization specifier group, which ought to be one of the %g, %e or %f designs for point numbers and %d for whole numbers.

The function returns 0 for success and GSL_EFAILED if there is an issue concerning the document.

int gsl_block_fscanf (FILE * stream, gsl_block * b): This function examines arranged information from the stream into the block b. The block b must be pre assigned with the right length since the function utilizes the size of b to decide what number of values to examine.

5.6. VECTORS

Vectors are characterized by a gsl_vector structure which depicts a cut of a square. Various vectors can be made which point to a similar square. A vector cut is a lot of similarly distributed component of an area of memory.

The gsl_vector structure contains five segments, the size, the step, a pointer to the memory where the components are stored, information, a pointer to the memory block of the vector and a block owning banner.

The structure is straightforward and resembles this, gsl_vector. The size is essentially the quantity of vector components. The scope of substantial lists runs from 0 to estimate 1. The step is the progression size starting with one component then onto the next in physical memory, estimated in units of the fitting data type.

The pointer information gives the area of the principal component of the vector in memory. The pointer block stores the area of the memory in which the vector components are found (assuming any).

In the event that the vector possesses this square, at that point the administrator field is set to one and the block will be located when the vector is free for allocation since vector allocation requires a few blocks to be free.

If the vector focuses to a block that stores some another information, at that point the proprietor field is zero and any hidden block won't be allocated with the vector. The functions for allotting and getting to vectors are characterized in gsl_vector.h.

5.6.1. Vector Allocation

The functions for dispensing memory to a vector follow the style of malloc. Moreover, they likewise play out their own error checking. If there is less amount of memory accessible to allocate a vector, at that point the functions call the GSL error handler (with an error number of GSL_ENOMEM) that helps in restoring an invalid pointer.

Thus, if one uses the library error handler to prematurely end the program, at that point it isn't important to check each alloc. gsl_vector * gsl_vector_ alloc (size_t n) This function makes a vector of length n, restoring a pointer to a recently introduced vector struct.

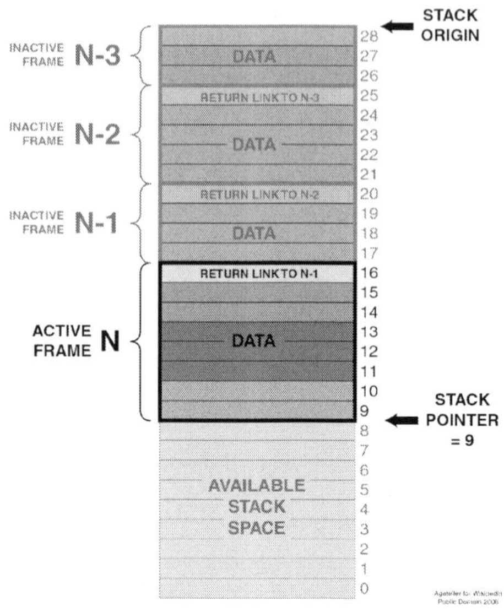

Figure 5.3. Vector allocation method.

Source: Image by Wikimedia.

Another block is distributed for the components of the vector, and provied in the block segment of the vector struct. The block is "claimed" by the vector, and will be deallocated when the vector is deallocated.

Zero-sized block allocation are substantial and return a valid outcome. gsl_vector * gsl_vector_calloc (size_t n) This function apportions memory for a vector of length n and instates all the components of the vector to zero. void gsl_vector_free (gsl_vector * v) This function liberates a formerly distributed vector v.

If the vector was made utilizing gsl_vector_alloc (), at that point the block hidden the vector will likewise be deallocated. If the vector has been made from another article, at that point the memory is still allocated to by that object and won't be deallocated.

5.6.2. Accessing Vector Elements

In contrast to Fortran compilers, C compilers don't offer help for checking of vectors and matrices. The functions gsl_vector_get() and gsl_vector_set() can perform versatile range checking and report an error in the event of the attempt to get to components outside the permitted memory.

The functions for getting to the components of a vector or matrix are characterized in gsl_vector.h and announced extern inline to dispense with work call overhead. One should incorporate the program with the preprocessor large scale HAVE_INLINE characterized to utilize these functions.

GSL_RANGE_CHECK_OFF in case of necessity one can kill run checking totally without changing any source documents by recompiling the program with the preprocessor definition GSL_RANGE_CHECK_OFF.

Given the compiler underpins inline functions the impact of killing extent checking is to supplant calls to gsl_vector_get(v,i) by v->data[i*v->stride] and calls to gsl_vector_set(v, i, x) by v->data[i*v->stride]=x.

In this way there ought to be no exhibition punishment for utilizing the range checking functions when range checking is killed. If one utilizes a C99 compiler which requires inline works in header documents to be pronounced inline rather than extern inline, characterizes the full scale.

With GCC this is chosen naturally when ordering in C99 mode (-std=c99). gsl_check_range If inline functions are not utilized, calls to the functions gsl_vector_get() and gsl_vector_set() will connect to the gathered adaptations of these functions in the library itself.

The range checking in these functions is constrained by the worldwide number variable gsl_check_range.

It is empowered as a matter of course to disable it, set gsl_check_range to zero. Because of function call overhead, there is less advantage in disabling range checking here than for inline functions. doublegsl_vector_get (const gsl_vector * v, const size_t I) This function restores the I-th component of a vector v.

If I lie outside the permitted scope of 0 to estimate – 1 then the error handler is summoned and 0 is returned. An inline form of this function is utilized when HAVE_INLINE is characterized. void gsl_vector_set (gsl_vector * v, const size_t I, double x) This function sets the estimation of the I-th component of a vector v to x.

If I lie outside the permitted scope of 0 to estimate – 1 then the error handler is conjured.

An inline version of this function is utilized when HAVE_INLINE is characterized. double * gsl_vector_ptr (gsl_vector * v, size_t I) const double * gsl_vector_const_ptr (const gsl_vector * v, size_t I). These functions return a pointer to the I-th component of a vector v.

In the event that I lie outside the permitted scope of 0 to measure – 1 then the error handler is conjured and an invalid pointer is returned. Inline forms of these functions are utilized when HAVE_INLINE is characterized.

5.6.3. Reading and Writing Vectors

The library gives functions to perusing and composing vectors to a record as double information or organized content. int gsl_vector_fwrite (FILE * stream, const gsl_vector * v) This function composes the components of the vector v to the stream in double organization.

The arrival esteem is 0 for progress and GSL_EFAILED if there was an issue contacting the record. Since the information is written in the local double arrangement it may not be compact between various structures. int gsl_vector_fread (FILE * stream, gsl_vector * v) This function adds extra block to the vector v from the open stream in double organization.

The vector v must be pre allotted with the right length since the function utilizes the size of v to decide what number of bytes to examine. The arrival esteem is 0 for progress and GSL_EFAILED if there was an issue perusing from the record (Figure 5.4).

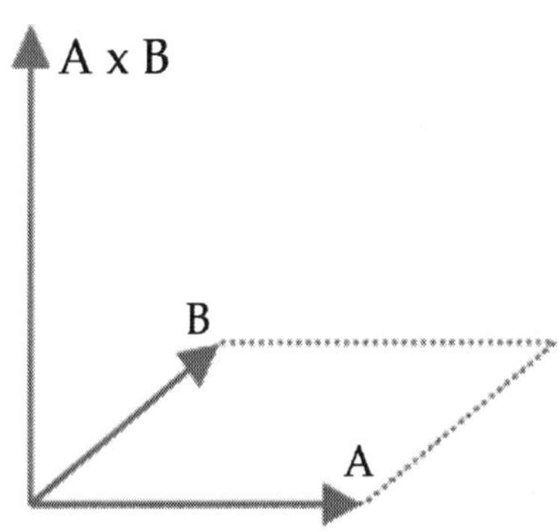

Figure 5.4. Reading and writing vectors.

Source: Image by Resumbrae.

The information is accepted to have been written in the local double configuration on a similar design. int gsl_vector_fprintf (FILE * stream, const gsl_vector * v, const roast * group) This function composes the components of the vector v line-by-line to the stream utilizing the organization specifier design, which ought to be one of the %g, %e or %f positions for drifting point numbers and %d for whole numbers. The function returns 0 for success and GSL_EFAILED if there was an issue concerning the document.

int gsl_vector_fscanf (FILE * stream, gsl_vector * v): This function examines designed information from the stream into the vector v. The vector v must be pre assigned with the right length since the function utilizes the size of v to decide what number to examine.

5.6.4. Vector Views

As the vectors can be created from block's pieces so it is also possible to create vector views by slicing vectors. For instance, a sub vector of another vector can be depicted with a view, or two perspectives can be made which give access to the even and odd components of a vector.

gsl_vector_view gsl_vector_const_view can be utilized to work on a subset of vector components. Vector perspectives can be characterized for both steady and non-consistent vectors, utilizing separate sorts that protect uncountability.

A vector has the sort gsl_vector_view and a steady vector has the sort gsl_vector_const_view. In the two cases the components of the view can become to as a gsl_vector utilizing the vector part of the view object. A pointer to a vector of type gsl_vector * or const gsl_vector * can be acquired by taking the location of this segment with the administrator.

When utilizing this pointer, it guarantees that the view itself stays in scope, the least complex approach to do so is by continually composing the pointer as &view.vector, and never putting away this incentive in another variable.

The beginning of the new vector is balanced by balance components from the beginning of the first vector. The new vector has n components. Scientifically, the I-th component of the new vector v 'is given by v'(i) = v->data[(offset + i)*v->stride] where the record I runs from 0 to n-1.

The information pointer of the returned vector struct is set to invalid if the consolidated parameters (balance, n) overwhelm the finish of the first vector. The new vector is just a perspective on the block hidden the first vector, v.

The block containing the components of v isn't possessed by the new vector. At the point when the view leaves scope the first vector v and its block will keep on existing. The first memory must be deallocated by removing the first vector. Obviously, the first vector ought not be deallocated while the view is still being used. The function gsl_vector_const_subvector() is comparable to gsl_vector_subvector() however, can be utilized for vectors which are pronounced.

const.gsl_vector_view

gsl_vector_subvector_with_stride(gsl_vector * v, size_t counterbalance, size_t stride, size_t n)

gsl_vector_const_viewgsl_vector_const_subvector_with_stride(const gsl_vector * v, size_t balance, size_t stride, size_t n)

These functions return a vector perspective on a sub vector of another vector v with an issue of extra step.

The sub vector is shaped similarly concerning gsl_vector_subvector() however, the new vector has n components with a stage size of step starting with one component then onto the next in the first vector.

Scientifically, the I-the component of the new vector v 'is given by v'(i) = v->data[(offset + i*stride)*v->stride] where the file I runs from 0 to n – 1. Note that sub vector realizes direct access to the hidden components of the first vector.

For instance, the accompanying code will zero the even components of the vector v of length n, while leaving the odd components immaculate: gsl_vector_view v_even = gsl_vector_subvector_with_stride (v, 0, 2, n/2); gsl_vector_set_zero (& v_even.vector); A vector view can be passed to any subroutine which takes a vector argument similarly as a directly allotted vector would be utilizing & view.vector.

For instance, the accompanying code figures the standard of the odd components of v utilizing the BLAS routine dnrm2:

gsl_vector_view

v_odd = gsl_vector_subvector_with_stride (v, 1, 2, n/2);

double r = gsl_blas_dnrm2 (&v_odd.vector); The function gsl_vector_const_subvector_with_stride() is proportional to gsl_vector_subvector_with_stride() however, can be utilized for vectors which are declared

const. gsl_vector_view

gsl_vector_complex_real (gsl_vector_complex * v) gsl_vector_const_view

gsl_vector_complex_const_real (const gsl_vector_complex * v)

These functions return a vector perspective on the genuine parts of the complex vector v. The function gsl_vector_complex_const_real() is proportionate to gsl_vector_complex_real() however, can be utilized for vectors which are declared.

const. gsl_vector_view

gsl_vector_complex_imag (gsl_vector_complex * v) gsl_vector_const_view

gsl_vector_complex_const_imag(const gsl_vector_complex * v)

These functions return a vector perspective on the nonexistent pieces of the complex vector v. The function gsl_vector_complex_const_imag() is comparable to gsl_vector_complex_imag() however, can be utilized for vectors which are declared

const. gsl_vector_view

gsl_vector_view_array(double * base, size_t n) gsl_vector_const_view

gsl_vector_const_view_array(const double * base, size_t n)

These functions return a vector perspective on an exhibit. The beginning of the new vector is given by base and has n components. Scientifically, the I-th component of the new vector v' is given by: v'(i) = base[i] where the list I runs from 0 to n-1.

The cluster containing the components of v isn't claimed by the new vector look. At the point when the view leaves scope the first exhibit will keep on existing. The first memory must be deallocated by liberating the first pointer base.

Obviously, the first cluster ought not be deallocated while the view is still being used. The function gsl_vector_const_view_array() is equal to gsl_vector_view_array() yet can be utilized for exhibits which are definite

const. gsl_vector_view_array_with_stride (double * base, size_t stride, size_t n)

gsl_vector_const_view gsl_vector_const_view_array_with_stride(const double * base, size_t stride, size_t n)

These functions return a vector perspective on a cluster base with an extra step contention. The sub vector is shaped similarly concerning gsl_vector_view_array () however, the new vector has n components with a stage size of step starting with one component then onto the next in the first exhibit.

Numerically, the I-th component of the new vector v 'is given by: v'(i) = base[i*stride] where the record I runs from 0 to n – 1. Note that the view gives direct access to the fundamental components of the first exhibit.

A vector view can be passed to any subroutine which takes a vector contention similarly as a legitimately assigned vector would be, utilizing &view.vector. The function gsl_vector_const_view_array_with_stride() is proportional to gsl_vector_view_array_with_stride() yet can be utilized for clusters which are proclaimed const.

5.7. QUBIT

A qubit is a quantum bit, a part in quantum registering to the paired digit or bit of traditional figuring. Similarly, as a part is the essential unit of data in a traditional computer, a qubit is the fundamental unit of data in a quantum computing.

In a quantum computing, various natural particles, for example, electrons or photons can be utilized (achievement has additionally been accomplished with particles), with either their charge or polarization going about as a portrayal of 0 as well as 1.

Every one of these particles is known as a qubit; the nature and conduct of these particles (as communicated in quantum hypothesis) structure the premise of quantum figuring. The two most pertinent parts of quantum physics are the standards of superposition.

Despite the fact that there are an unbounded number of conceivable qubit values, watching a qubit's state by making a quantum estimation yields either 0 or 1. The aftereffect of a given estimation is probabilistic and relies upon the restraints of this combination.

Qubits with values on the equator of the circle are similarly prone to be 0 or 1 when estimated, yet they are largely extraordinary. As the bolt follows a way along the equator, various types speak to stage contrasts, numbers liable for resistance impacts when two qubits unite.

5.7.1. Representing a Qubit

Zero and one is the value which a binary digit or a bit can have, on the other hand 0 and 1 can be the value a qubit that is either of these or a quantum superposition of 0 and 1. With the help of two-dimensional column vector of unit norm, the state of a single qubit can be described, which means, the total sum should be 1 of the magnitude formed of its entries (Figure 5.5).

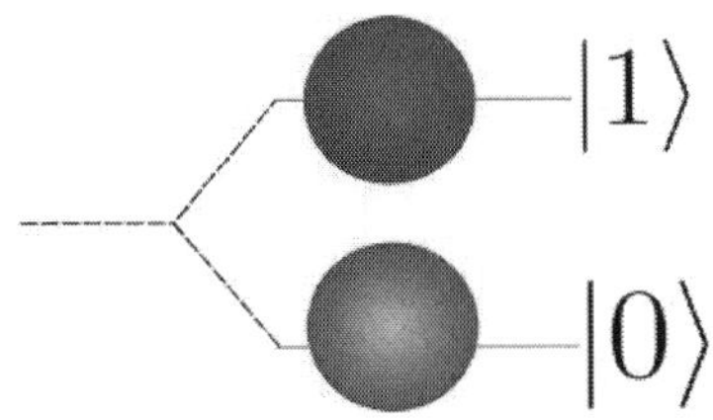

Figure 5.5. Simple qubit representation.

Source: Image by Wikimedia.

This vector will be referred as the quantum state vector. Quantum state vector is the one which helps to describe the one-qubit quantum system, as it holds all the information needed. It describes in a way like just as a single bit holds all of the information needed to describe the state of a binary variable.

With the norm 1 of any two-dimensional column vector of real or complex numbers w represents a possible quantum state which is held by a qubit. Therefore, with the help of [αβ] qubit state is represented and if α and β are considered as the complex numbers which is satisfying $|\alpha|^2+|\beta|^2=1$.

[10] and [01] are considered as the quantum state vectors which take a special role. For the vector space these two vectors form a basis which describes the qubit's state. This implies any quantum state vector can be composed as an aggregate of these premise vectors.

In particular, the vector [xy] can be composed as x [10] + y [01]. While any revolution of these vectors would fill in as a consummately substantial reason for the qubit, one can decide to benefit this one, by considering it the computational premise.

We take these two quantum states to relate to the two conditions of a previous bit, to be specific 0 and 1. The standard show is to pick 0≡[10], 1≡[01], 0≡[10], 1≡[01], despite the fact that the contrary decision could similarly well be taken.

Consequently, out of the infinite number of conceivable single-qubit quantum state vectors, just two compare to conditions of previous bits; all other quantum states don't compare.

5.7.2. Measuring a Qubit

Since it is realized how to represent a qubit, one can increase some instinct for what these states represent by talking about the idea of estimation. An estimation relates to the casual thought of observing the qubit, which quickly falls the quantum state to one of the two old states [10] or [01].

At the point when a qubit given by the quantum state vector [αβ] is estimated, one can get the result 0 with likelihood $|\alpha|^2$ and the result 1 with likelihood $|\beta|^2$. On result 0, the qubit's new state is [10]; on result 1 its state is [01]. Note that these probabilities summarize to 1 as a result of the standardization condition $|\alpha|^2+|\beta|^2=1$.

The properties of estimation additionally imply that the general indication of the quantum state vector is unimportant. Discrediting a vector is comparable to $\alpha \rightarrow -\alpha$ and $\beta \rightarrow -\beta$.

Since the likelihood of estimating 0 and 1 relies upon the extent squared of the terms, embeddings such signs do not change the probabilities at all. Such stages are normally called worldwide stages and also it can be of the structure eiϕeiϕ instead of just ±1.

A last significant property of estimation is that it doesn't really harm all quantum state vectors. If one start with a qubit in the state [10], which relates to the old state 0, estimating this state will consistently yield the result 00 and leave the quantum state unaltered.

In this sense, if one just has traditional bits (i.e., qubits that are either [10] or [01]) at that point estimation doesn't harm the framework. This implies one can reproduce traditional information and control it on a quantum computer similarly as one could do on an old computer.

The function, nonetheless, to store data in the two states on the double is the thing that lifts quantum processing past what is possible traditionally and further plunder quantum computers of the function to duplicate quantum information unpredictably.

5.8. VISUALIZING QUBITS AND TRANSFORMATIONS

Qubits may likewise be imagined in 3D utilizing the Bloch circle representation. The Bloch circle gives a method for portraying a solitary qubit quantum state (which is a two-dimensional complex vector) as a three-dimensional real valued vector. This is significant on the grounds that it permits us to picture single qubit states and along with that it creates thinking that can be important in comprehension multi qubit states (where the Bloch circle representation separates).

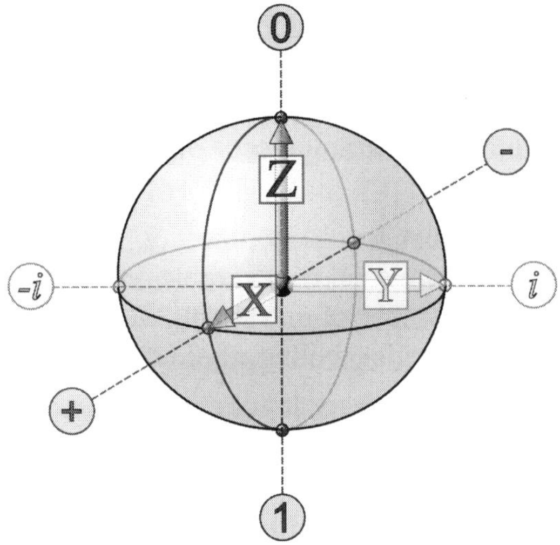

Figure 5.6. Qubit Bloch sphere.

Source: Image by Freesvg.

While considering a quantum calculation as an arrangement of turns is an incredible instinct, it is trying to utilize this instinct to plan and depict calculations. Q# resolves this issue by giving a language to portraying such revolutions.

5.8.1. Single-Qubit Operations

Quantum computers process information by applying an all-inclusive arrangement of quantum entryways that can copy any revolution of the quantum state vector.

This idea of comprehensiveness is similar to the thought of all-inclusiveness for conventional (i.e., traditional) computing where a gate set is viewed as general if each change of the info bits can be performed using a limited length circuit.

In quantum computing, the legitimate changes that one is permitted to perform on a qubit are unitary changes and estimation. The adjoint activity or the unpredictable conjugate transpose is of urgent significance to quantum computing since it is expected to reverse quantum changes.

Q# mirrors this by giving strategies to consequently incorporate entryway successions to their adjoint, which spares the software engineer from giving

consistent entryways are vital for quantum calculation, particularly at the quantum calculation configuration level. To accomplish deficiency lenient equipment execution, they will eventually be accumulated into discrete entryway successions that intently rough these revolutions.

5.8.2. Multiple Qubits

While single-qubit entryways have some irrational highlights, for example, the function to be in more than one state at a given time, in the event that all one had in a quantum computer were single-qubit gates, at that point one would have a device with computational force that would be overshadowed by even an adding machine like an old supercomputer.The genuine intensity of quantum computing just gets obvious as the increment in quantity of qubits. This force emerges, to a limited extent, in light of the fact that the component of the vector space of quantum state vectors develops exponentially with the quantity of qubits (Figure 5.7).

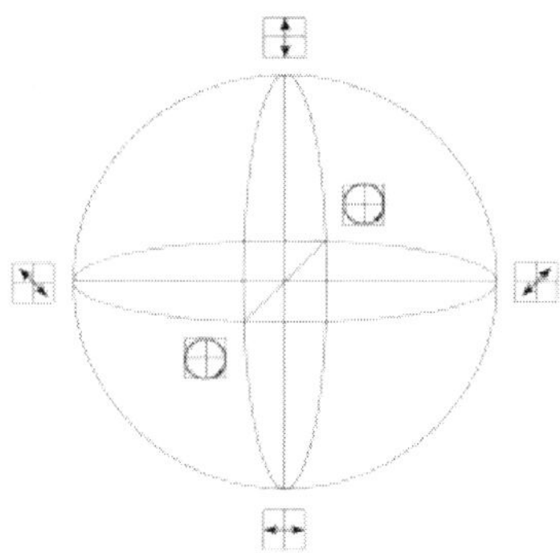

Figure 5.7. Multiple qubit representation.

Source: Image by Wikimedia.

This implies while a solitary qubit can be inconsequentially demonstrated, recreating a fifty-qubit quantum calculation would apparently push the restrictions of existing supercomputers. Expanding the size of the calculation by just a single extra qubit copies the memory required to store the state and generally pairs the computational time.

This quick multiplying of computational force is the reason a quantum PC with a moderately modest number of qubits can far outperform the most impressive supercomputers of today, tomorrow, and past for some computational undertakings.

For what reason do one have exponential development for quantum state vectors? The objective in this segment is to audit the standards used to construct multi-qubit states out of single-qubit states just as talk about the entryway tasks that one has to remember for their gate set to frame an all-inclusive many-qubit quantum computer.

These devices are completely important to comprehend the gate sets that are regularly utilized in Q# code and furthermore to pick up instinct regarding why quantum impacts, for example, resistance render quantum computing more remarkable than old computing.

5.9. MATRICES

Matrices are characterized by a gsl_matrix structure which depicts a summed up cut of a block. Like a vector it represents a lot of components in a region of memory, yet utilizes two records rather than one.

gsl_matrix

The gsl_matrix structure contains six segments, the two elements of the matrix, a physical measurement, a pointer to the memory where the components of the matrix are stored with information, a pointer to the block used by the matrix block, assuming any, and a block owning banner.

The physical measurement decides the memory design and can contrast from the matrix measurement to permit the use of submatrices. Matrices are stored in push significant request, implying that each line of components frames alongside a block in memory.

This is the standard "C-language requesting" of two-dimensional clusters. Note that Fortran stores clusters in segment significant request. The quantity of lines is size1. The scope of legitimate line lists runs from 0 to size1-1. Essentially size2 is the quantity of sections.

The scope of legitimate segment lists runs from 0 to size2 – 1. The physical line measurement tda, or trailing measurement, indicates the size of a column of the matrix as spread out in memory. For instance, in the accompanying matrix size1 is 3, size2 is 4, and tda is 8.

The physical memory format of the matrix starts in the upper left hand-corner and continues from left to directly along each line. Each unused memory area is represented by "XX." The pointer information gives the area of the main component of the matrix in memory.

The pointer block stores the area of the memory block in which the components of the matrix are found (assuming any). If the matrix possesses this block, at that point the proprietor field is set to one and the block will be deallocated when the matrix is free.

In the event that the matrix is just a cut of a block possessed by another item then the proprietor field is zero and any basic block won't be freed. The functions for apportioning and getting to matrices are characterized in gsl_matrix.h.

5.9.1. Matrix Allocation

The functions for distributing memory to a matrix follow the style of malloc. They additionally play out their own error checking.In case, if there is deficient memory accessible to designate a matrix, at that point the functions call the GSL error handler (with an error number of GSL_ENOMEM) notwithstanding restoring an invalid pointer.Therefore, if one uses the library error handler to prematurely end the program, at that point it isn't important to check each alloc. gsl_matrix * gsl_matrix_alloc (size_t n1, size_t n2) This function makes a matrix of size n1 pushes by n2 segments, restoring a pointer to a recently instated matrix struct.

Another block is assigned for the components of the matrix, and put away in the block part of the matrix struct. The block is "claimed" by the matrix, and will be deallocated when the matrix is deallocated.

Mentioning zero for n1 or n2 is substantial and restores a non-invalid outcome. gsl_matrix * gsl_matrix_calloc (size_t n1, size_t n2) This function distributes memory for a matrix of size n1 pushes by n2 sections and introduces all the components of the matrix to zero.void gsl_matrix_free (gsl_matrix * m) This function releases a formerly designated matrix m. In the event that the matrix was made utilizing gsl_matrix_alloc() at that point the block hidden the matrix will likewise be deallocated. If the matrix has been made from another item, at that point the memory is as yet claimed by that object and won't be deallocated.

5.9.2. Reading and Writing Matrices

The library gives functions to perusing and composing matrices to a document as parallel information or organized content. int gsl_matrix_fwrite(FILE * stream, const gsl_matrix * m) This function composes the components of the matrix m to the stream in paired arrangement.

The arrival approval is 0 for progress and GSL_EFAILED if there was an issue contacting with the document. Since the information is written in the local parallel group it may not be compact between various models.

int gsl_matrix_fread(FILE * stream, gsl_matrix * m) This function adds something extra to the matrix m from the open stream in double configuration. The matrix m must be reallocated with the right measurements since the function utilizes the size of m to decide what number of bytes to examine.

The arrival esteem is 0 for progress and GSL_EFAILED if there was an issue perusing from the record. The information is accepted to have been written in the local paired configuration on a similar design.

int gsl_matrix_fprintf (FILE * stream, const gsl_matrix * m, const burn * design) This function composes the components of the matrix m line-by-line to the stream using the organization specifier group, which ought to be one of the %g, %e or %f positions for scanning point numbers and %d for whole numbers.

The function returns 0 for success and GSL_EFAILED if there was an issue concerning the document.

int gsl_matrix_fscanf (FILE * stream, gsl_matrix * m): This function examines organized information from the stream into the matrix m. The matrix m must be reallocated with the right measurements since the function utilizes the size of m to decide what number of numbers to examine.

5.9.3. Matrix Views

A matrix view is a transitory object, stored in the stack, which can be applied to work on a subset of matrix components. Matrix perspectives can be characterized for both consistent and non-steady matrices utilizing separate sorts that save uncountability.

A matrix see has the sort gsl_matrix_view and a consistent matrix see has the sort gsl_matrix_const_view. In the two cases, the components of the view can be got to utilizing the matrix segment of the view object.

A pointer gsl_matrix * or const gsl_matrix * can be acquired by taking the location of the matrix with the administrator. Notwithstanding matrix views, it is similarly conceivable to make vector perspectives on a matrix, for example, line or segment views.

These functions return a matrix perspective on a submatrix of the matrix m. The upper-left component of the submatrix is the component (k1, k2) of the first matrix. The sub matrix has n1 lines and n2 segments. The physical number of sections in memory given by tda is unaltered.

The new matrix view is just a perspective on the block basic the current matrix, m. The block containing the components of m isn't used by the new matrix view. At the point when the view leaves scope the first matrix m and its block will keep on existing.

The first memory must be deallocated by removing the first matrix, once its work is done. Obviously, the first matrix ought not be deallocated while the view is still being used. The function gsl_matrix_const_submatrix() is identical to gsl_matrix_submatrix() however, can be used for matrices which are declared const.

These functions return a matrix perspective on the group base with a physical number of sections tda which may vary from the comparing measurement of the matrix. The matrix has n1 lines and n2 segments, and the physical number of segments in memory is given by tda.

The new matrix is just a perspective on the exhibit base. At the point when the view leaves scope the first cluster base will keep on existing. The first memory must be deallocated by removing the first group once its work is done. Obviously, the first group ought not be deallocated while the view is still being used.

The function gsl_matrix_const_view_array_with_tda () is equal to gsl_matrix_view_array_with_tda () however, can be used for matrices which are declared const.

5.10. CONCLUSION

In this chapter, the concepts of vectors and matrices have been described. The process of matrix and vector allocation are important and plays an essential role in the computer programming. The process of reading and writing of vectors, blocks, and matrices have also been elaborated in an efficient manner.

Due the fact that vector is used in 1D either as an array or pointer in computing programming. It is essentially a part of the computer graphics that are used in the graphical programming systems.

The concept of qubit described in this chapter, is an essential concept in the field of quantum computing since numerical procedures are used mostly in the quantum computing it was essential to describe its functions and working which has been done considering the use of vectors and matrices in it.

Hence, the procedures of single and multiple qubits have been described. The conclusion can be made from the study is that it is essential for the computing programming to understand the effectiveness of vectors and matrices.

REFERENCES

1. Docs.microsoft.com. (2017). *Vectors and Matrices in Quantum Computing-Microsoft Quantum*. [online] Available at: https://docs.microsoft.com/en-us/quantum/concepts/vectors-and-matrices (accessed on 4 June 2020).
2. Gnu.org. (n.d). *Vectors and Matrices—GSL 2.6 Documentation*. [online] Available at: https://www.gnu.org/software/gsl/doc/html/vectors.html (accessed on 4 June 2020).
3. Hardesty, L., (2013). *Explained: Matrices*. [online] MIT News. Available at: http://news.mit.edu/2013/explained-matrices-1206 (accessed on 4 June 2020).
4. Mathworks.com. (2020). *Matrices, Vectors, And Scalars- MATLAB & Simulink*. [online] Available at: https://www.mathworks.com/help/comm/ug/matrices-vectors-and-scalars.html (accessed on 4 June 2020).
5. Trccompsci.online. (n.d). *Vectors-Trccompsci-AQA Computer Science*. [online] Available at: https://www.trccompsci.online/mediawiki/index.php/Vectors (accessed on 4 June 2020).

CHAPTER

6

SOLUTIONS OF EQUATIONS, INTERPOLATION, AND APPROXIMATION

CONTENTS

In this chapter, there is a discussion about errors and approximations in numerical methods. The different type of errors in numerical methods has been discussed in this chapter. In this chapter, the errors in numerical computation and approximations in numerical analysis has also been discussed in this chapter.

In this chapter, the errors and their propagation and solutions of linear algebraic equations has been discussed in this chapter. In this chapter, the numerical solutions of equations by iteration methods and Aitken technique for interpolation has also been discussed in this chapter.

6.1. ERRORS AND APPROXIMATIONS IN NUMERICAL METHODS

The errors from different sources can enter in a numerical process. Many errors can be avoided entirely while others can be inevitable and can only be reduced. It is also important to consider the way various errors occur, the way they advance in the process and the way the quality of the tests is compromised due to errors.

6.1.1. Modeling Error

The physical process or event is showed by creation of a mathematical model. In the final solution, errors that appear if a mathematical model is getting developed is also not precise or accurate in comparison with the ongoing physical operation.

The models also need several suppositions which simplify them. In certain instances, the physical mechanism under modeling can be excessively complex. For these cases, constructing an accurate mathematical model will be difficult and impractical. Therefore, the resulting model can be a condensed version of the actual mechanism behind its process.

Some examples of model simplification, resulting in errors:

1. In determining the strength that operates on a freely falling body, the drag coefficient (air resistance) may be believed to be linearly proportional to the speed of the falling body. The simplification may impact the precision of the result. When measuring the force on a freely moving body, the drag coefficient (air resistance) can be considered to be linearly proportional to the height of the falling body. This simplification can affect the precision of the outcome.

2. In the assessment of outbreak control systems, epidemiological considerations are primarily used in the model and socioeconomic factors and others may be omitted to make the process less complex.

The fundamental input for a numerical method is the mathematical model. Thus, the numerical process cannot produce correct results that match the physical system if the model is misconception.

In order to reduce this flaw, they should develop the model and add complexities to the code. Growing the difficulty of the model makes it easier to solve the algorithm and allows the software solution more computing power to use. The over extrapolation of the model, on the other hand, simplifies the counting process, which results in inadequate amounts of precision.

The level of accuracy required to achieve the results and the complexity level of the model must also be balanced. The model must only be improved to an appropriate degree by means of an improvement in complexity.

6.1.2. Inherent Errors or Input Errors

The inherent errors are errors in the data that are manually entered into the model. It is also known as input errors. These are divided in two-errors in data errors and conversion errors.

6.1.2.1. Data Errors

Whenever the data (to be incorporated into a model) is collected by using experimental methods then there is probability of an error and this error is known as scientific errors.

These errors occur mainly because of the instrumentation limitations or mistakes. The precision of the voltmeter determines the accuracy of the reading of voltage. In the same manner, the efficiency of measuring distance is restricted through the precision of the device utilized measure distance.

It is however, very necessary to improve the quality of the data interpreted rather than the accuracy of arithmetic operations in order to decrease these errors.

6.1.2.2. Conversion Errors

The computers have fixed storage capacity to keep in memory the precise decimal data that cause the errors in conversion. This are thus considered errors in representation. The computer can only keep a finite number of digits in a floating-point representation. The n Non-retained estimates contribute to rounding errors.

There are many numbers that cannot not be accurately represented if a floating-point number is changed into its binary form.

The floating-point number 0.1, for example, transforms into a binary form that does not end. In computer memory the 0.1 goes through an error as there is decrease in the number of decimal numbers. The frequency of the mistake grows as arithmetic operations are done over and over for these numbers. The result will not be 1 when 0.1 is sum over ten times in this instance.

6.1.3. Numerical Errors

The errors can occur during the process of numerical method implementation. Therefore, they are often called procedural errors. They are graded into two errors-Round-off and Truncation errors.

The cumulative number error in a method can be determined as the sum of round-off errors and in-line truncation errors. Taking these variables into consideration, effective methods may be implemented to reduce the overall numerical error during the execution of a numerical system.

6.1.3.1. Round off Error

The fixed capacity to store precise figures by computers cause round off errors. In a numerical method, these errors will have a cumulative effect. The round-off error occurs after the same number has been recorded. In each operation, round-off error might happen, and these errors sum up as repetitive arithmetic operations are carried out. The total rounding error might become important because of the cumulative effect following repetitive arithmetical operations as the initial rounding errors are insignificant.

It can be classified into two parts:

1. **Chopping:** The numbers which are outside the computer's storage space are lost in chopping error. The number such as 10.6872 will be saved as 10.68 if the computer word length is 4 digits. It is going to be dropped in figures 7 and 2.
2. **Symmetric Round Off:** The last relevant digit maintained in a symmetric round-off is rounded off by 1, if the first digit is more than or equal to 5 then the last relevant digit maintained in a symmetric round-off is rounded off by 1. The last remaining digit is unchanged, although it is lower than 5.

The number 10.6872 would become 10.69 in the case above, since 7 is more than 5. The number will be saved as 10.68 if the original number is 10.6842.

6.1.3.2. Truncation Error

If an exact method in mathematics is accurately measured then truncation error happens. This often occurs when an infinite number of series must be applied to achieve the exact outcome, but due to practical problems they have to break off the process after they have achieved a reasonable level of accuracy. The truncation error happens as a numerical method is overwritten after a finite number of equation simplicity iterations.

The infinite numbers must be added to achieve the result in computation of sin of a value, of an exponential function. They generally break the numerical cycle following a long number of terms due to computational constraints and create a truncation error.

A stronger numerical model, that typically increases the amount of arithmetically worked, will minimize truncation error. For instance, the number of points in which the feature is implemented can decrease the truncation error. However, sensitivity should be given to ensure that the round-off error attributed to an improvement in arithmetic functions does not account for a decrease in truncation error.

They typically use the library functionality to measure logarithms, exponentials, trigonometric, hyperbolic functions, etc. The sequence is being utilized to test these capacities in all these situations. Knowing the truncation mistakes caused by these library functions is critical.

6.1.4. Human Errors

That is attributed to mistakes or imperfections created by human beings. In any level of the process of problem solving, human errors can happen. These are some typical errors

The lack of a mathematical equation or a model which does not adequately represent the structure analyzed that is Modeling error

- choosing a flawed computational method;
- Failure to consider the problem or physical system;
- It overlooks certain fundamental assumptions needed to formulate the model or making incorrect assumptions that is Modeling error;
- Choose an erroneous algorithm for the numerical process use;

- Programmable errors;
- Code entry errors like the misprints, providing column-like values to a vector, not a row wise, etc.; and
- There is a mistake in assumption of wrong values.

Initial errors can be eliminated with a good knowledge of the problem and the procedure for numerical solution, the use of reliable programming methods and tools, successful code analysis and checking. Both of these errors are preventable.

6.2. ERROR IN NUMERICAL COMPUTATION

Error: In numerical analysis to calculate things numerically they have to make approximations. They can set limits and get correct answers in calculus, however, they cannot take an infinite limit when they utilize a computer, take a simple thing, like a derivative, to estimate the response and then have an error. The potential of computers for precision and quantity of numbers is minimal.

In measures and estimates, they should describe errors with respect to their frequency and precision. The close correlation between a measured value and the real value is defined as accuracy. The near similarity of measured values to each other is defined as precision. Inaccuracy is the deliberate divergence from the actual values often known as bias is called inaccuracy. Imprecision (also known as uncertainty) refers to The extent of close relationship between calculated results is known as imprecision or uncertainty. The inaccuracy and imprecision in the results is shown by the concept of error.

Round-off Error: The computers are not able to signify certain quantities is the cause of happening of round off error. It is important to know the round off error because it may lead to incorrect results. It can even give rise to an unstable calculation that clearly produces incorrect results in some situations. These are known as ill-conditioned calculations.

The numerical calculations are generally involved in two important aspects of round-off error

- Computers are able to store and calculate the magnitude and precision limits on their numbers.
- Some numerical calculations are highly susceptible to round-off

errors. This can be done both from the mathematical structure of the calculations from the way the computers perform the work.

6.2.1. Computer Representation of Integers

The computer systems that use a hardware binary representation for the integral values usually have one out of two options available to them for the effective representation of negative integers- that is one's complement or two's complement.

In general, the high-order bit of a binary representation is applied as a sign bit. For example, if the value is 11, then the number is negative, while on the other hand, if the value is 00, the number is non-negative.

In a computer system that uses one's complement notation, the representation of a negative number is the one's complement of the representation of a positive number. Alternatively, it can be said that the negation of an integer can be done by excluding its value with a word consisting of all 1's. hence, in one's complement, assuming a 4-bit word for compactness.

1 = 0001

4 = 0100

-1 = 1110

-2 = 1101

As its name implies, two's complement, represents negative integers by taking their complement in regards to the next higher power of 22. Therefore, in a 44-bit world, the negative of a value is found by subtracting it from 2525 (as a bit string). For example, 1=00011=0001, so −1=10000−0001=1111-1=10000-0001=1111.

An unfortunate outcome of using one's complement notation is that zero has two distinct representations:

0=0000=11110=0000=1111

Two's complement fixes this, since −0=10000−0000=10000-0=10000-0000=10000, which gets truncated in 4 bits to 00000000. Although, it introduces an asymmetry in the representational range. Whereas, a 44-bit one's complement number can represent any integer from −7-7 to +7+7, a 44-bit two's complement number can represent integers from −8-8 to +7+7, −8-8 being represented by the value 10001000.

In addition to that, in certain cases, the two's complement is more natural as compared to the one's complement since if you regard the representation as an unsigned number, its value modulo 2wordsize is in fact the value it represents. In other words, for example, consider again a 44-bit word size. Then the representation of −2-2 in two's complement is 11101110. Thinking of 11101110 as an unsigned number, its value is 1414, which is in fact −2(mod24).

This means that, the multiplication of two's complement representations is bit easy - one just need to multiply the bit patterns together as if they were unsigned, and consider the rightmost bits of the result (thus taking the result modulo the word size).

No such simple algorithm is possible by using one's complement notation, Thus, for example, in one's complement one has-

-1 = 1110

-2 = 1101

2 = -1 . -2 = 0010

yet multiplying the unsigned values and truncating results in 01100110, or 66.

6.2.2. Computer Representation of Floating-Point Numbers

A floating-point number, also known as real number can represent a very large (1.23×10^88) or a very small (1.23×10^-88) value. It could also be used to represent a very large negative number (-1.23×10^88) and very small negative number (-1.23×10^88), as well as zero. This is shown below:

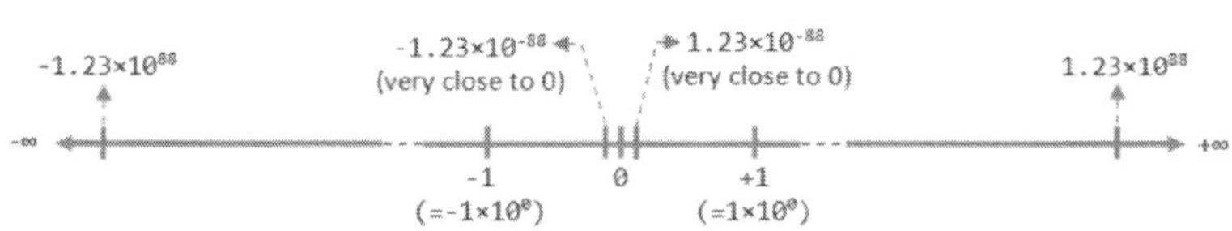

Floating-point Numbers (Decimal)

A floating-point number is generally expressed in the scientific notation, with a fraction (F), and an exponent (E) of a certain radix (r), in the form of F×r^E. while the decimal numbers use radix of 10 (F×10^E); and binary numbers use radix of 2 (F×2^E).

The computer representation of floating-point number is not unique. Let us take an example to understand- the number 55.66 can be represented as 5.566×10^1, 0.5566×10^2, 0.05566×10^3, and so on. The fractional part can be normalized and in the normalized form, there is only a single non-zero digit before the radix point. For instance, decimal number 123.4567 can be normalized as 1.234567×10^2; binary number 1010.1011B can be normalized as 1.0101011B×2^3.

It is really crucial to note that the floating-point numbers suffer from a loss of precision when they are represented with a fixed number of bits (for example- 32-bit or 64-bit). The main reason behind this is that there are infinite number of real numbers (even within a small range of says 0.0 to 0.1). while, on the other hand, a n-bit binary pattern can represent a finite 2^n distinct numbers. As a result, not all the real numbers can be represented. Instead of this, the nearest approximation will be used, that will eventually result in loss of accuracy.

In addition, it is important to note that floating number arithmetic is very much less efficient as compared to the integer arithmetic. It could be speed up with a so-called dedicated floating-point co-processor. Thus, it is suggested to use integers if the application does not require floating-point numbers.

In computers, floating-point numbers are represented in scientific notation of fraction (F) and exponent (E) with a radix of 2, in the form of F×2^E. Both E and F can be positive as well as negative. Modern computers adopt IEEE 754 standard for representing floating-point numbers. There are two representation schemes: 32-bit single-precision and 64-bit double-precision.

In 32-bit single-precision floating-point representation:

- The most significant bit is the sign bit (S), with 0 for positive numbers and 1 for negative numbers.
- The following 8 bits represent exponent (E).
- The remaining 23 bits represents fraction (F).

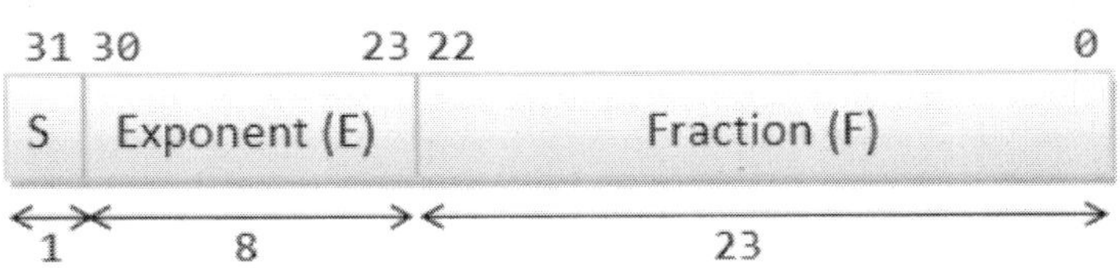

32-bit Single-Precision Floating-point Number

The representation scheme for 64-bit double-precision is almost similar to the 32-bit single-precision:

- The most significant bit is the sign bit (S), with 0 for positive numbers and 1 for negative numbers.
- The following 11 bits represent exponent (E).
- The remaining 52 bits represents fraction (F).

64-bit Double-Precision Floating-point Number

6.2.2.1. Truncation Error

Truncation errors are defined as those that result from using an approximation in place of an exact mathematical procedure.

Let us see an example of approximation to a derivative using a finite-difference equation:

$$\frac{dv}{dt} \cong \frac{\Delta v}{\Delta t} = \frac{v(t_{i+1}) - v(t_i)}{t_{i+1} - t_i}$$

Another example can be of Taylor series. According to the Taylor theorem, any smooth function can be approximated as a polynomial. The Taylor series gives a means to express this idea mathematically, as-

$$f(x) = f(x_0) + \frac{1!}{x - x_0} f'(x_0) + \frac{2!}{(x - x_0)_2} f''(x_0) + \cdots + \frac{n!}{(x - x_0)_n} f_{(n)}(x_0) + R_n$$

Usually, the nth order Taylor series expansion will be the same for an nth order polynomial. In some other cases, the remainder term Rn is of the order of hn+1, which means-

- The more terms are used, the smaller the error, and
- The smaller the spacing, the smaller the error for a given number of terms.

6.3. THE APPROXIMATIONS IN NUMERICAL ANALYSIS

There are range of difficulties that are posed by mathematical problems that are emerging from scientific applications that prevent the scientist in resolving them precisely. In order to achieve approximate solutions, this has

led to an increasingly broad range of methods for calculating approximations of quantities that exist in such problems. The types of approximations and the various techniques in assessing e accuracy of these approximations.

6.3.1. Sources of Approximation

It should be supposed that individual is trying to solve a problem that emerges out of a technical application's mathematical model. It is said that this problem is well-positioned because it fits the following conditions.

- There is a particular solution of a problem;
- If there is any type of small change in problem data then it contributes to a small change of the solution that is, the solution constantly depends on the results;
- The process of solving a well-positioned problem can be seen by first condition as equal to evaluating some function 'f' at a certain known value x, in which x specifies the problem details. Because familiarity with function f is restricted in many situations, the role of computing f(x) can be perceived, at minimum in principle, as the implementation of certain potentially infinite sequence of steps which solves the underlying problem for data x; and
- For numerical analysis the objective is for the computation of an equation f(x) by a finite series of steps from an algorithm.

In the course of computing this approximation to f(x), two general forms of error occur:

- The error in the data a is called data error. The numerical assessment involves addressing an estimated data problem x with a problem in actual. The exact statistics are always inaccessible, as measurements or other estimates that are unreliable because of insufficient precision must be collected. Moreover, data should be changed such that the solution process can be simpler.
- The error that happens while attempting to calculate f(ˆx) is called computational error. In actual reality, f(x) must be approximated by Ãf(x), where Ãf is a function approximating f. The consequence of this approximation may be a truncation occurring when a finite sequence of steps does not precisely evaluate f, so a finite sequence which evaluates f approximately should be employed instead.

6.3.1.1. Basics of Error Analysis

At all times, it is not impossible to infer that a variety of approximations can be used in any statistical estimate, which each carry a calculated solution error. The impact of these approximations on precision will also be understood. The study of these results is known as the assessment of errors.

1. Forward Error and Backward Error

It should be presumed that the value y = f(x) approximation = y = f(x) for that function f and given the problem data x. = f(x). There should be a clearly defined concept of error in such an approach until they can evaluate the accuracy of this method.

This exact description is given below- Definition (Forward error) Let x be a real number and f: R is a feature, let R be a feature. If y = is an actual number approximating y = f(x), the forward error in Δy = $\hat{y}$ − y is the difference.

If y is not equal to 0, relative forward error in $\hat{y}$ is defined by-

$$\frac{\Delta y}{y} = \frac{\hat{y} - y}{y}$$

Obviously, in error analysis, our primary objective is to achieve an estimation of the forward error Δy. Sadly, this calculation can be hard to obtain directly.

Alternatively, to treat the measured value as the precise answer to a transformed data problem, i.e. $\hat{}$ = f(x) where ˆx is a perturbation of x.

2. Backward Error Description

Let x be real and let f: R can be R to be a function. Assume that y, the real number of y = f(x), y = f; that is to say, y = f(a) is the approximation of y = f(x) for any real number of x = f. Next, the values is Δx = $\hat{x}$ − x is backward error in $\hat{y}$. When x is not equal to 0, the relative forward error in yˆ is described as-

$$\frac{\Delta x}{x} = \frac{\hat{x} - x}{x}$$

The evaluation process of Δx is known as backdated error assessment. It has been observed that As we can see, this approximation of the backward error can be used to approximation the forward error in accordance with information about f. The floating-point arithmetic does not obey actual arithmetic rules. It makes it impossible to evaluate forward error. However, actual arithmetic is used in backward error analysis, as the measured answer is supposed to be the right solution to a changed problem. The preference given to backdated error analysis is might be due to this. In round off error assessment, it is presumed that fl(x op y) = (x op y)(1 + δ), in which op is an arithmetic method, and that δ is an unknown constant that satisfies |δ| ≤ mach. The relative error in fl(x op (y) is can be seen from this inference. The relative reverse error in every operand is also |δ| in the case of the addition.

3. Sensitivity and Conditioning

The objective of error analysis is, in almost all of the situations, to achieve an estimation of the forward relative error (f(ax) − f(x))/f(x), although it is also better to measure the relative backward error (ax − x)/x instead. Hence, the forward error must be calculated in terms of the backward error. The need is discussed in the following definition.

i Definition of Condition Number

Let suppose x be a real figure and let f be a function: R/R. The absolute condition number, indicated by κabs, is the ratio of the scale of the forward error to the scale of the backward error the absolute condition number, denoted by κabs,

$$k_{abs} = \frac{|f(\hat{x}) - f(x)|}{|\hat{x} - x|}$$

If f(x) is not equal to 0, the relative state number of the computational problem y = f(x) is the ratio of the magnitude of the relative forward error to the magnitude of the relative backward error, -

$$k_{rel} = \frac{|(f(\hat{x}) - f(x)) / f(x)|}{|(\hat{x} - x)/x|} = \frac{|\Delta y / y|}{|\Delta x / x|}$$

Any state number is logically a calculation of the solution change caused by a change in the information. Although the relative number of conditions appears to be a more accurate indicator of this transition, it is often alluded to it as merely the number of conditions.

The minor shift in the data will create a relatively significant difference in the solution if the condition large is large and it is assumed that the situation is either absolute or vulnerable. If the amount of the condition is minimal then it is assumed that the problem is either well-conditioned or insensitive.

The condition number must be calculated in order to determine the relative forward error because the condition number, as per previous statement, rely on the knowledge of the exact solution f(x). For this purpose, for the sake of convenience, that f: R → R is differentiable and obtain-

$$
\begin{aligned}
k_{rel} &= \frac{|x\Delta y|}{|y\Delta x|} \\
&= \frac{|x(f(x+\Delta x)-f(x))|}{|f(x)\Delta x|} \\
&\approx \frac{|xf'(x)-\Delta x|}{|f(x)\Delta x|} \\
&\approx \frac{|xf'(x)|}{|f(x)|}
\end{aligned}
$$

Moreover, if the backward error¨error Δx can be approximated and if they can bind f and f' close to x, the condition number can be bonded, and the relative forward error can be calculated. It is true that, if the exact value f(x) is zero, then the condition number is unknown. The absolute condition number can be utilized in this instance. The absolute state number can be calculated using the derivative of f, using the same method as before. In fact, they have got κabs ≈ |f' (x)|.

ii Conditioning, Stability, and Accuracy

The issue is essential in the error assessment of an algorithm to solve the problem, to determine the state or sensibility of a problem, but it does not provide enough details to decide whether an algorithm is going to provide a precise approximate solution.

Note that a function f's condition number depends, among other things, on the absolute forward error f(æx) − f(x). In addition, a f(x) evaluation algorithm evaluates a function −f approximating f-generating a − =¨f(x) approximation to the exact y = f(x) solution. It has been presumed that f(x)=f (x) is the exact solution to an adjacent problem for a certain ˆx which is near to x; that is the estimated answer to the initial problem is the exact solution.

This presumption has enabled to specify the condition number of f regardless of any estimation ˆf. This independence is important, since a problem's sensitivity depends solely on the problem itself, and not on any algorithm that can be used to solve it roughly. Is it always fair to conclude that an estimated solution to a nearby problem is the real answer.

Though it is not a case. There may be a potential for unnecessarily sensitive disruption of a data algorithm that produces an exact approximation to other data. This corresponds to the idea of a balanced algorithm, an algorithm applied to a given data x problem is secure when a rough solution is determined and is an exact solution to a given data x problem, where x is a little x disturbance.

The measured solution may be considered reliable in that the relative error in the computed solution is small if a problem are well defined and if a stable algorithm to solve them is available. It can be seen that the correct solution cannot be predicted by a stable algorithm for the ill-conditioned problem.

6.4. ERRORS AND THEIR PROPAGATION

Some of the most effective features of electronic digital computer numerical analysis systems is that it almost always produces numbers. Due to the tremendous efficiency of the machines, it is normal to look with a certain air of infallibility at the outcomes of their calculations. The findings can only be the analytical and programming method used by the machine, and these are the work of an incredibly flawed individual.

The garbage in garbage out idiom has originated because of this. The small mistakes can quickly spread to large ones at any particular stage which destroy the validity of the result as machines perform the large number of equations.

The computational errors can be divided into two general categories; the round off error is the first one and the truncation errors the second. Maybe the most subtle of the two is a total mistake and it's still present at some point. Its existence is also representative of the first issue that is being faced. In their functions, digital computers use some amount of numbers and the base number of numbers is known as machine precision.

Sometimes the number of digits may be multiplied or tripled and thus the term double or triple precision is widely used to denote a measurement performed using this extended number of digits. It's normal practice to use more The digits being used more than the issue required is a general practice to make sure the digit is right. There is a slight problem for the scientist in this, since the desire to report all the digits provided by the machine is typically tremendous. Therefore, scientific papers frequently include numerical results comprising of far more decimal places than explained by the measurement or that had gone into the problem. The full precession of the system is never justified, since the last digit value would generally be somewhat unknown after the first arithmetic measurement. It is the product of the first form of error that they term round-off error.

The computer with just one significant number and the measurement exponent such that 6 + 3 that gives 9×100 can be taken as an instance. Nevertheless, 6 + 4, 6 + 5, and 6 + 8 will all give the same answer, notably 1×101. The other information will be lost, as the machine carries just one digit. The results of 6 + 9 or 7 + 9 are not immediately apparent.

If the result is 2 to 101, the calculations will be completed by the computer at the next big digit. If the result is 1 to 101, however, then the computer will be expected to cut off the addition to the closest significant digit. How the device actually does depend on the machine's physical architecture that is hardware and the programs that is software that direct it to perform the task. If a human operator does the calculation, it is generally possible to see what happens and to make that possible by holding more important figures, but this is typically not the scenario for computers.

It is very important to focus on taking care of the concern that the round-off error is propagated to the final computer outcome. It's tenting to suggest that the example above is only impossible for a 1-digit machine. The common 6-digit machine can be given thought though. It'll not be able to differentiate between $1 million and $1 million and $9. The zero will be obtained if these two numbers are subtracted.

To any bank accountant, this would be relevant. The first digit is completely insignificant due to repetitive operations of this kind. The issue as to how precise an answer is required is emphasized in it.' They actually require ample numbers for the account to take care of all the money at the rates the bank has agreed upon.

The Internal Revenue Service, for instance, encourages taxpaying citizens to round all figures to the nearest dollar in the united states of America. It limits the number of meaningful digits to a lower limit. The earnings normally determine the upper limit. The very fewer universal constants in the physical universe are considered to have more than four digits in that light speed is a rare exception.

There is nothing more significant than four figures in the outcome of physical modeling. There are exceptions once again, such as zero studies, but scientists do not necessarily assume that their results are improved than they are. The comprehensive research was dedicated to this subject by assuming that round-up errors occur in a random fashion.

While computers are essentially deterministic that is the computer will still reach at the same result provided that same initial state, a large set of arithmetic operations may be considered to generate a random array of round-ups and round-downs. The number of digits affected can also vary, however, making it much more difficult to analyze the issue as a whole.

6.5. SOLUTIONS OF LINEAR ALGEBRAIC EQUATIONS

Knowledge is also arranged around rows and columns in science, industry, and mathematics to create rectangular arrays called matrices. Matrices are often present as tables of numerical results, but often in various statistical forms, which are derived from empirical observations. Such a matrix has all the necessary details to overcome a particular equations structure.

In order to solve equation systems, the computer programs a created since computers are well suited to manage numerical knowledge arrays. Matrices, however, are not just a method to solve equation schemes, they can be considered as mathematical structures by themselves, and a philosophy rich and significant with a multitude of functional applications is connected with them.The mathematical field, that is denoted as linear algebra, is focused on the analysis of matrices and related topics. Owing to the advent of computers and computer information systems, the terminology and principles of linear algebra and matrix methods have been widely used in many fields of research and engineering over the preceding 300 years.

The applications in various areas including signal processing, sensors, finites, connectivity, computer vision, electromagnetics, health sciences and social science, have been successfully applied to matrices.

6.5.1. Gaussian Elimination Method and Gauss Jordan Method

The computational science powerhouse for the solution of a linear equation system is called Gaussian elimination method. The algorithm for the linear equations solving structures and determining a matrix rank and calculating the inverse of an invertible square matrix is done by Gaussian elimination in linear algebra.

The German mathematician and Carl Friedrich Gauss the scientist is honored by naming this equation. The technique was discovered independently in Europe by Carl Friedrich Gauss in his 1809 publication Theory of Motion of Celestial Bodies, when he developed the least squares technique.

The transforming of the coefficient matrix in to an upper triangular matrix, solves a given equation system in n variables and the n solves the unspecified by back substitution in a gauss elimination method.

Method to Solve: There are two sections in Gaussian elimination method. The first element (Forward Elimination) The decrease of a given system to either triangular or echelon form is done by the first part or forward elimination, then it change into a depraved equation without solution, implying that there is no solution to the problem.

This is achieved by using Elementary. The backward substitution to find the device solution above is used in second stage. In elementary row operations, the first component reduces an echelon-shaped matrix to row echelon form, and the second decrease it to the reduced row echelon form, or canonical shapes of rows.

For the given method, write row, in the (n+2) Nd column, the sum of the coefficients in each row. The operation should also be done on the same operation on column elements. The row sum element in (n+2)nd row will then be equivalent to the total of the components of the respective transformed row at any point in the lack of computational errors.

Algorithm for Gaussian Elimination: The augmented matrix columns should be changed one by one into the triangular echelon shape. The existing column is referred to as the pivot board. Then start from left to right, and let the first column be the pivot column, and next the second column, and then, prior to the actual vertical line, the last column. In order to find a diagonal element in the pivot column for each pivot column, do two steps before moving to the next pivot column.

The pivot is called this element. The pivot row is referred to as the row comprising the pivot. Then each pivot element in the pivot row should be divided by pivot to obtain a new pivot row with a 1 in the place of pivot.

The subtracting of a correct multiple of the pivot row from each of the rows under it should be done to get in each place zero.

When this process has been completed, the enhanced matrix is in triangular echelon form and can be solved by back substitution.

The steps of Gauss elimination method:

For linear equations system compose the augmented matrix.

In order to turn A into the upper triangular form, use the elementary row operations on the augmented matrix [A|b]. If the null is on the diagonal, move the rows till a null is in that position. If it is not possible to do then stop, it has endless or no solution. In order to get answer to a problem the method of back substitution should be applied.

The Systems of Linear Equations:

1. **Gaussian Elimination:** The solving of nonlinear equation systems is quite complicated, whereas linear solutions are very easy to study. There are computational methods that aim to compare nonlinear systems against linear models with the expectation that linear systems solutions may be very much same to nonlinear systems solutions.

The equation is -

$a x + b y + c z + d w = h$

The known numbers in this are a, b, c, d, and h, whereas unknown numbers are x, y, z, and w, is called a linear equation. The linear equation is said to be homogeneous if h=0.

The series of linear equations is called linear system and a linear system which is homogeneous is a series of linear equations that are homogeneous.

The following example display the method to solve the system of equations by gaussian elimination.

The series of Elementary Row Operations should be carried out on augmented matrix. Set the column pivot to column 1. In diagonal position put 1. Then put 0's under the pivot: let the column pivot = second column now. p Firstly, put a 1 in the place of the diagonal: then get a 0 in the place underneath the pivot: let the column pivot Equal the third column. Have a 1 in the diagonal place: this matrix, now in the shape of a triangular echelon, reflects: it is solved by method of the back substitution. The replacing of $z = 3$ from the third equation to the second equation yields $y = 5$ and replacing $z = 3$ and $y = 5$ to the first equation yields $x = 7$. So, the complete solution is: $\{x = 7, y = 5, z = 3\}$.

2. **Gauss Jordan Method:** Another type of variation of gauss elimination is gauss Jordan method. Once, the coefficient matrix is being converted into another matrix that is much easy to solve, and the structure portrayed by the new augmented matrix has the same solution set as the original linear equation structure.

The main target is of changing the matrix coefficient into a diagonal matrix in gauss Jordan elimination and one column at a time, the zeros are added into the matrix. During one move through the matrix, they work to delete the elements both above and below the diagonal portion of a given column.

Solving Method-

The process in Gauss-Jordan elimination method are:

For linear equations system compose the augmented matrix.

To transform A into diagonal form, using elementary row operations on the augmented matrix [A]. If there is a zero on the diagonal, move the rows until there is a nonzero at that position. If you can't, stop; the program has unlimited solutions, or no solutions.

Render each diagonal element equal to one by splitting the diagonal element and the right-hand-side element in each row by diagonal element in that row.

Many individuals prefer Gauss-Jordan Elimination over Gaussian Elimination when doing calculations by hand, as it eliminates the need for back replacement. However, we can later prove that elimination of Gauss-Jordan requires a little more effort than elimination of Gaussian, and hence it is not the tool of choice for solving systems of linear equations on a machine.

This linear equation systems which contain two or more variables can be solved by this method. The system has to be modified to an expanded matrix though.

The inverse of a 2×2 matrix or larger matrices, 3×3, 4×4 can be discovered by the use of this matrix.

In this case, it should be observed that in order to find the matrix must be a square.

The system of linear equations can be answered but the use of augmented matrix.

a1 x + b1 y + c1z = d1

a2 x + b2 y + c2 z = d2

a3x + b3 y + c3z = d3

System of Equations *f*

Augmented Matrix *f*a1 b1 c1 d1

a2 b2 c2 d2

a3 b3 c3 d3

If an equation method is given, the coefficients of each variable must be taken and placed into a matrix, to be written in an augmented matrix form.

In this example, in the following system:

$3x + 2y - z = 3$

$x - y + 2z = 4$

$2x + 3y - z = 3$

3 2-1 3

Augmented matrix ƒ1 -1 2 4

2 3 -1 3

Through the use of Gauss-Jordan elimination process at the time of solving or decreasing a matrix there is application of three different operations that re called elementary row operations.

1. The two rows are interchanged;
2. The one row should be added to another one, or first multiply one row, after that add to another; and
3. The operation of multiplication should be carried out on Multiply a row by any constant exceeding zero.

The identity matrix is the final result obtained by decreasing the equation. This matrix consists of the first number in the diagonal. The numbers in the final section are the solutions to the equations system are the numbers in the last column.

1 0 0	3	
0 1 0	2	←âŽ¯âŽ¯Identity Matrix for a 3×3
0 0 1	5	
1 0 0 0	2	
0 1 0 0	6	←âŽ¯âŽ¯Identity Matrix for a 4×4
0 0 1 0	1	
0 0 0 1	4	

The same pattern is applied for bigger matrices.

Solving a system using Gauss-Jordan

The best way to go is to get the ones first in their respective column, and then using that one to get the zeros in that column. It is very important to understand that there is no exact procedure to follow when using the Gauss-Jordan method to solve for a system.

3x + 2y – z = 3

x – y + 2z = 4

Write as an augmented matrix.

2x + 3y – z = 3

6.6. NUMERICAL SOLUTION OF EQUATIONS BY ITERATION

In order to obtain a numerical solution of the equation f(x) = 0 with an iteration, an approximative solution is first found and a more precise solution is then used. This cycle is replicated until a solution is identified to the degree of accuracy needed.

For example, Newton showed that you can find the square root of a number a from the iteration equation Xi+l = 1/2 (Xi + a/xi). I = 0, 1, 2, etc. Where Xo is the estimate from which iteration starts. So, we move ahead as follows, in order to find a sequence of estimated values of; 2, each with increasing precision. Let xo = 1·5-find bisection method by the first point.

$$x_1 = \frac{1}{2}\left(x_0 + \frac{a}{x_0}\right) = 0.5(1.5 + 2/1.5) = 1.4166...$$

Then, this value is used to locate Xz. The value of x2 is calculated to be = 1·4142 when rounding x1 to 1·4167.

$$x_2 = \frac{1}{2}\left(x_1 + \frac{a}{x_1}\right) = 0.5(1.4167 + 2/1.4167) = 1.4142...$$

The accuracy of similar extent as in the bisection process has only been accomplished in two steps.

1. **Using a Spreadsheet:** Using a spreadsheet this basic iteration process is achieved more effectively. The table that to use is Microsoft Excel, although all commercial spreadsheets have same function. Launch the spreadsheet and insert and click Insert

in cell A1. Here they insert the numbers for iteration in this first column.

Write 0 and press Enter in cell A2. In cell A2, put the cell highlight and highlight the cell block A2 to A7 with the mouse button kept down and the highlight washed off at the cell A7. Click on the Top bar Edit button and point at fill from the down menu. From the next Dropdown menu, choose Series and approve 1 by default, by clicking OK in the Series window. The numbers 1 to 5 are lined in cells A3 to A7.

In the cell B1, insert letter x-the successive x values generated from iteration in this column will be included. In cell B2, enter Xo's value, that is, 1·5. The number in cell B3 is 1·416667 and then enter the formula= 0·5*(B2 + 2/B2).

Position the highlight of the cell in cell B3, press the Edit button on the Command panel, and choose Copy from the drop-down menu. The formula has now been copied into the clipboard in cell B3. Outline the B4 to B7 cells and then press the Edit button though and choose Paste this time from the drop-down menu. The B4 to B7 cells fill the screen with numbers

X	n
5·1	0
416667·1	1
414216·1	2
414214·1	3
414214·1	4
414214·1	5

The view can be changed to include the following by using the different formatting facilities given by the spreadsheet

n	x
0	1•500000000000000
1	1•416666666666670
2	1•414215686274510
3	1•414213562374690
4	1•414213562373090
5	1•414213562373090

There are 15 decimal positions. There that are significantly higher than average, which illustrate how accurate a can be a spreadsheet. Remember that it is necessary to replicate the iterations until there is no shift in the outcome from one iteration to the next to consider a meaning equivalent to a given number of decimal positions or relevant figures. Save the file with an appropriate name like Newton, because it can be use again.

2. **Relative Addresses:** In cell B3, position the cell highlight and the formula found therein is = 0·5*(B2 + 2/B2). Then put the cell spotlight in cell B4, and = 0·5*(B3 + 2/B3) is the formula.

In the formula in B3, as you insert the cell address B2 the spreadsheet recognizes it to represent the cell contents directly above. This concept is copied into cell B4 where B3 is the cell directly above.

When you want to refer to a particular cell in a system so an absolute address must be used. In Cell C1 position the cell highlight and insert the number 2. Then put the cell spotlight in cell B3 and re-enter the formula = 0·5*(B2+C1/B2) and copy it into B4 to B7 cells.

The numbers in the second column do not alter but the calculations do as the same relation to cell Cl is made in cells B3 to B7. The dollar signs have been used to signify an actual address. To get a show, change the number in cell C1 to 3, as shown below-

n	x
0	1•500000000000000
1	1• 750000000000000
2	1•732142857142860
3	1•732050810014730
4	1•732050807568880
5	1•732050807568880

These are the iterated J3 values the square root of cell Cl content.

6.7. AITKEN TECHNIQUE FOR INTERPOLATION

In the computer program the Aitken techniques can be implemented in an easier way and thus are famous techniques of interpolation.

With regard to (n+1) points (x0, y0), (x1, y1)., (xn, yn) (n+1) points (x0, y0), (x1, y1)., (xn, yn) in which the x values do not generally need to be spaced in an equal manner. It is assumed that to seek value of y at a given value of x:

The interpolation polynomial of degree 1 in the very first phase of approximation is as follows

$$\Delta_{01}(x) = \frac{1}{x_1 - x_0}\begin{vmatrix} y_0 & x_0 - x \\ y_1 & x_1 - x \end{vmatrix}$$

$$\Delta_{02}(x) = \frac{1}{x_2 - x_0}\begin{vmatrix} y_0 & x_0 - x \\ y_2 & x_2 - x \end{vmatrix}, \text{ etc.}$$

The interpolation polynomial of degree 2 in the very second phase of approximation is as follows:

$$\Delta_{012}(x) = \frac{1}{x_2 - x_1}\begin{vmatrix} \Delta_{01}(x) & x_0 - x \\ \Delta_{02}(x) & x_2 - x \end{vmatrix}$$

$$\Delta_{013}(x) = \frac{1}{x_3 - x_1}\begin{vmatrix} \Delta_{01}(x) & x_1 - x \\ \Delta_{03}(x) & x_3 - x \end{vmatrix}, \text{ etc.}$$

The interpolation polynomial of degree 2 in the very second phase of approximation is as follows:

$$\Delta_{0123}(x) = \frac{1}{x_3 - x_2}\begin{vmatrix} \Delta_{012}(x) & x_2 - x \\ \Delta_{013}(x) & x_3 - x \end{vmatrix}, \text{ etc.}$$

The interpolation technique interpolation technique is as follows:

x	y	Stage1	Stage2	Stage3
x_0	y_0			
		$\Delta_{01}(x)$		
x_1	y_1		$\Delta_{012}(x)$	
		$\Delta_{02}(x)$		$\Delta_{0123}(x)$
x_2	y_2		$\Delta_{013}(x)$	
		$\Delta_{03}(x)$		
x_3	y_3			

In the above example, the value of y at a given value of x can be calculated from somewhere between 0123(x) and 0123(x).

For example:

Find f(0.25) using Aitken interpolation technique from the following data:

CHAPTER
7

NUMERICAL SOLUTIONS TO ORDINARY AND PARTIAL DIFFERENTIAL EQUATIONS

CONTENTS

The chapter numerical solutions to the ordinary differential equations and partial differential equations explains the meaning of a differential equations. This chapter also explains the several numbers of various methods in which an ordinary differential equation can be solved or how can an individual determine the approximate solution to that particular differential equation.

This chapter provides highlights on the Taylor series method with numerical derivatives for numerical solution of ordinary differential equations initial value problems. This chapter also explains the working of Euler's method. This chapter also addresses the Runge Kutta method and Numerov's method in order to find the approximate solution of an ordinary differential equation.This chapter also includes the several numbers of various partial differential equations such as first order partial differential equation, as well as the second order partial differential equation. This chapter also explains the semi linear and non-linear partial differential equations.

7.1. AN INTRODUCTION TO ORDINARY DIFFERENTIAL EQUATIONS

The definition of an ODE (short form for Ordinary Differential Equation) is that, an equation in which some of the ordinary derivatives (are opposite of the partial derivatives) of a function. Every so often, the main objective is to find out the solution of an ordinary differential equation (ODE), that is, in order to find out what function or functions fulfils the equation or satisfies the equation.If an individual or a person knows, what is the derivative of a function is, how can he or she find the function itself? The person is required to find out the anti-derivative, that is, he or she need to integrate that particular equation. For instance, if an individual is given by

$dx/dt\ (t) = \cos t$

With respect to this case, what is the function of x (t)? Since the anti-derivative of the cost t is sin t, in this way, x (t) must be sin t. Apart from that, an individual forgot one vital point. There is always an arbitrary constant that no person can able to find out, if he or she only knows the derivative. In this way, all can be found out from the equation that is mention above is that

$x\ (t)=\sin t + C$

for some arbitrary constant C. An individual or a person can cross check that indeed x (t) fulfils the equation of

$dx/dt = \cos t.$

Generally speaking, through the course of solving an ODE, which is more complexed part of integration when it is compared with the simple integration. Never the less, the basic ideology or basic principle is always integration, as it is required to go from the derivative to the function.

Typically, the more challenging task or more challenging part is to find out that what integration is required to do.

7.1.1. The Simplest Possible ODE

Let's begin from the simple part. What could be the simplest possible ODE? Let x (t) be function of t, which fulfils the ODE:

$$dx/dt = 0 \qquad (1)$$

An individual or a person can ask some very simple questions such as, what is x (t)? is x (t) distinctly find out from this particular equation? And if not, then apart from this, what do he or she need to specify?

Looking at equation number (1) which means that x (t) is a constant function, x (t) = C. It is certainly not distinctly identified, as there is no other methodology in order to specify the constant C if an individual or a person only have equations for the derivatives of x. In order to distinctively find out the value of x (t), one must provide some additional information or data with respect to the function x (t) itself.

For instance, specifying the value of x (t) must be equivalent to 31 when the value of t is equals to 11, addition the condition

$$x(11) = 31$$

only after then, an individual or a person will be found out the value of the arbitrary constant, that is C which is equals to 31. And the function is x (t) = 31 for all values of t. An individual frequently thinks of the variable t as representing time and refer to a condition, for example x (11) = 31 as an initial condition.

Let's write down the initial condition more generally as

$$x(t_0) = x_0,$$

in which, t_0 depicts some give time, and x_0 depicts some given number. It is as though, that an individual initializes the system which is to be equal with the number x_0 at given interval of time $t = t_0$. Never the less, this "initial condition" also finds out the value of x (t) for early times.

As it can be seen that from the solution x (t) = 31 for all time t, this condition lay down the state of the system for times before and after t = 11.

7.1.2. A Slightly More Complicated ODE

Let' make things a little more complex. Taking the equation

$$dx/dt = m \sin t + n t^3 \qquad (2)$$

in which, m, and n depicts some real numbers. From the equation number (2), it is not much complicated when it is compared with the equation number (1). And the reason behind that is that, the right-hand side does not rely of value of x.

Right hand side only rely on the value of t. It is just stipulating what the derivates is in terms of t. The solution is just the antiderivative, or the integral.

Now, let's do the integration part slightly different. This time, using the definite integral from time t = a to time t = b. With the help of fundamental theorem of calculus, the integral of dx/dt from a to b must be in the form of

$x(b) - x(a) = \int_a^b dx/dt = \int_a^b (m \sin t + n t^3)\, dt = - m \cos b + n b^4/4 - (- m \cos a + n a^4/4)$.

In this way, the solution can be written in several numbers of different ways. The value of b can be replaced with an arbitrary time t,

$x(t) = - m \cos t + n t^4/4 + m \cos a - n a^4/4 + x(a)$.

This form makes it very obvious how the solution x(t) would rely on an initial condition $x(t_0) = x_0$. If x (7) = 5, then

$x(t) = - m \cos t + nt^4/4 + m \cos 7 - n7^4/4 + 5$.

On the contrary, if an individual or a person is not concerned with the type of the constant, he or she could just write the general solution in the form of,

$x(t) = - m \cos t + n t^4/4 + C$

for some arbitrary constant C.

7.2. TAYLOR SERIES METHOD WITH NUMERICAL DERIVATIVES FOR NUMERICAL SOLUTION OF ODE INITIAL VALUE PROBLEMS

The Taylor series method is one of the earliest analytic-numeric algorithms in order to approximate the solution of the initial value problems in the context of ODEs.

In the present interval of time, this algorithm is not applied so much. And the reason behind this is that, when an individual is trying to solves systems of ODEs, evaluating the higher order of derivatives formally is an overelaborate task, this is true even if an individual or a person uses the computer algebraic system, for example, MATHEMATICA or MAPLEV.

Apart from this, the other reason is that, only the explicit versions of this algorithm are known. The primary idea of the restoration of these sorts of algorithm is based on the approximate calculation of the higher derivatives with the help of a well-known technique for the partial differential equations (PDEs).

With respect to some cases, these sorts of algorithms will be much more complex when it is compared with the Runge Kutta methods. And the reason behind this that, it will necessitate more function evaluation when they are compared with the well-known classical algorithms.

Never the less, these sorts of evaluations can be achieved entirely parallel and the coefficients of truncated Taylor series can be evaluated with the help of matrix-vector operations. With respect to large systems these sorts of operation suit for the parallel computers.

These types of algorithms have several numbers of various beneficious characteristics over the extensively used classical methods. The approximate solution is given as a piecewise polynomial function which is defined on the subinterval of the entire interval as well as the local error of this solution at the interior points of the subinterval is less than that one at the end point.

This characteristic provides a distinct facility with respect to the adaptive error control. It has been remarked that, for the explicit Taylor series methods is possible in order to give its implicit extension. With the help of this fact, that the approximate solution is a continuous function, (with respect to the case of implicit version it is a continuously differentiable function), adaptive examination and control of some qualitative properties of the algorithms will be much simpler when it is compared with the case when the approximate solution are given only at discrete grid points.

$y' = f(x, y)$

$y(x_o) = y_o$

an individual or a person chose upon what interval, beginning at the initial conditions, he or she require to determine the solution. He or she can reduce the interval into small sub-division of length, denoted with the help of 'h.' after then, with the help of initial condition as the starting point, he or she can generate the rest of the solution with the help of the iterative formulas, as shown below:

$x_{n+1} = x_n + h$

$y_{n+1} = y_n + h\, f(x_n, y_n)$

in order to find out the coordinates of the points in the numerical solution. One has to terminate this process when he or she have reached the right end of the required interval.

7.3.1. A Preliminary Example

Just to get a feel for the method in action, let's work a preliminary example completely by hand. Let's assume that, an individual or a person was asked to solve the initial value problem:

$Y' = x + 2y$

$y(0) = 0$

numerically, finding a value for the solution at $x = 1$, and using steps of size $h = 0.25$.

7.3.2. Applying the Method

Obviously, the explanation of the problem points toward that the interval he or she will be finding a solution on is [0, 1]. The differential equation given tells the formula for f (x, y) required with the help of the Euler Method, namely:

$f(x, y) = x + 2y$

and the initial condition expresses the values of the coordinates of the starting point:

- $x_o = 0$
- $y_o = 0$

now, with the help of the Euler method formulas, in order to generate values for x_1 and y_1.

The x-iteration formula, with $n = 0$ gives:

$x_1 = x_o + h$

or:

$x_1 = 0 + 0.25$

So:

$x_1 = 0.25$

And the y-iteration formula, with n = 0 gives the equation as:

$y_1 = y_o + h\,f(x_o, y_o)$

or:

$y_1 = y_o + h\,(x_o + 2y_o)$

or:

$y_1 = 0 + 0.25\,(0 + 2*0)$

In this way:

$y_1 = 0$

Summarizing, the second point in the numerical solution is:

- $x_1 = 0.25$
- $y_1 = 0$

now move on to get the next point in the solution, (x_2, y_2).

The x-iteration formula, with n = 1 gives the equation as follows:

$x_2 = x_1 + h$

or:

$x_2 = 0.25 + 0.25$

So:

$x_2 = 0.5$

And the y-iteration formula, with n = 1 gives the equation as follows:

$y_2 = y_1 + h\,f(x_1, y_1)$

or:

$y_2 = y_1 + h\,(x_1 + 2y_1)$

or:

$y_2 = 0 + 0.25\,(0.25 + 2*0)$

So:

$y_2 = 0.0625$

Summarizing, the third point in our numerical solution is:

- $x_2 = 0.5$
- $y_2 = 0.0625$

now move on to get the fourth point in the solution, (x_3, y_3).

The x-iteration formula, with n = 2 gives the equation as:

$x_3 = x_2 + h$

or:

$x_3 = 0.5 + 0.25$

So:

$x_3 = 0.75$

And the y-iteration formula, with n = 2 gives the equation:

$y_3 = y_2 + h\,f(x_2, y_2)$

or:

$y_3 = y_2 + h\,(x_2 + 2y_2)$

or:

$y_3 = 0.0625 + 0.25\,(0.5 + 2*0.0625)$

So:

$y_3 = 0.21875$

Summarizing, the fourth point in the numerical solution is:

- $x_3 = 0.75$
- $y_3 = 0.21875$

now move on to get the fifth point in the solution, (x_4, y_4).

The x-iteration formula, with n = 3 gives the equation as follows:

$x_4 = x_3 + h$

or:

$x_4 = 0.75 + 0.25$

So:

$x_4 = 1$

And the y-iteration formula, with n = 3 gives the equation:

$y_4 = y_3 + h\,f(x_3, y_3)$

or:

$y_4 = y_3 + h\ (x_3 + 2y_3)$

or:

$y_4 = 0.21875 + 0.25\ (0.75 + 2*0.21875)$

So:

$y_4 = 0.515625$

Summarizing, the fourth point in the numerical solution is:

- $x_4 = 1$
- $y_4 = 0.515625$

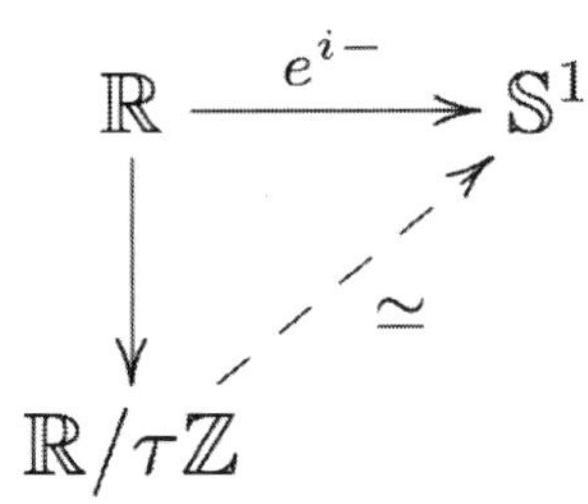

Figure 7.1. An illustration of Euler's formula.

Source: Image by Wikipedia.

7.4. RUNGE KUTTA METHODS

In the previous Euler's Method, the information is being used on the slope or the derivative of y at the given time step in order to generalize the solution with respect to the next time-step. The LTE (short form for Local Truncation Error) for the method is $O(h^2)$, as an outcome in a first order numerical technique.

Runge-Kutta methods are a class of methods. In which, carefully uses the information on the 'slope' at more than on point in order to generalize the solution with respect to the future time step. First of all, let's discuss the first derivative of the second order Runge Kutta method, in which LTD is $O(h^3)$.

$k_1 = h\ f\ (y_n, t_n)$

$k_2 = h\ f\ (y_n + \beta\ k_1, t_n + \alpha h)$

$y_{n+1} = y_n + a\ k_1 + b\ k_2,$ (1)

in which, the constants α, β, a, and b have to be assessed, in such a way that outcome method has a LTD of $O(h_3)$. Consider that, if k_2=0 and a=1, then Equation number (2) reduces to the forward Euler method.

Now, let's write down the Taylor series expansion of y in the neighborhood of t_n correct to the h^2 term that is,

$$y(t_{n+1}) = y(t_n) + h\,(dy/dt)\,t_n + (h^2/2 * d^2y/dt^2)\,t_n + O(h^3) \qquad (2)$$

Never the less, from the IVP (Initial Value Problems)that dy/dt = f(y, t) so that

$$d^2y/d\,t^2 = df(y, t)/dt = df/dt + df/dy * dy/dt = df/dt + f\,(df/dt)$$
(3)

In this way, from the above analysis, that is, with the help of Equation number (2) and (3), the equation will be

$$y_{(n+1)} = y_n + hf\,(y_n + t_n) + h^2/2\,[df/dt + f\,(df/dy)\,]\,(y_n, t_n) + O(h^3)$$
(4)

Never the less, the term k_2 in the proposed Runge Kutta method of Equation number (2) can be expanded correct to $O(h^3)$ in such a way that

$$k^2 = hf\,(y_n + \beta\,k_{1,}\,t_n + \alpha h)$$

$$= h\,[f\,(y_n, t_n) + \alpha h\,(df/dt)\,(y_n, t_n) + \beta\,k_1(df/dt)\,(y_n, t_n)] + O(h^3)$$
(5)

Now, substituting for k_2 from Equation number (2), then the equation will be

$$y_{(n+1)} = y_n + (a + b)\,h\,f\,(y_n, t_n) + b\,h^2\,[\alpha\,(df/dt) + \beta\,f\,(df/dt)\,(y_n, t_n) + O(h^3) \qquad (6)$$

Now, comparing the terms which are having the same coefficients from the Equation number (5) and then equation number (7) gives the following system of equations in order to find out the constants:

$$a + b = 1$$

$$\alpha\,b = 1/2$$

$$\beta\,b = 1/2. \qquad (7)$$

There are several numbers of various choices of a, b, α and β which fulfils the equation number (7). For instance, choosing $\alpha = \beta = 1$and a=b=1/2. With respect to this choice, the classical second order accurate Runge-Kutta method (Runge Kutta 2) which is summarized as follows.

$$k_1 = h\,f\,(y_n, t_n)$$

$$k_2 = h\,f\,(y_n + k_1, t_n + h)$$

$y_{n+1} = y_n + (k_1 + k_2)/2$, Second Order Runge-Kutta Method (Runge Kutta 2). (8)

In same way, Runge-Kutta methods of higher order can also be generated. One of the most extensively used methods in order to find out the solution of initial value problems is the fourth order Runge-Kutta (RK4) technique. The LTD of this method ish[5] The method is given below.

$k_1 = h f(y_n, t_n)$

$k_2 = h f(y_n + k_1/2, t_n + h/2)$

$k_3 = h f(y_n + k_2/2, t_n + h/2)$ Fourth Order Runge-Kutta Method (Runge Kutta 4).

$K_4 = h(y_n + k_3, t_n + h)$

$$y_{n+1} = y_n + (k_1 + 2k_2 + 2k_3 + k_4)/6. \quad (9)$$

Application Problem

1. In this program for Runge Kutta method in C, a function f (x, y) is defined to calculate slope whenever it is called. F (x, y) = (x – y)/(x + y)

SOLUTION:

```
#include <stdio.h>
# include <math.h>
float f (float x, float y);
void main ()
{
float x0, y0, m1, m2, m3, m4, m, y, x, h, xn;
print f (“Enter x0, y0, xn, h:”);
scanf(“%f %f %f %f,”&x0,&y0,&xn,&h);
     x = x0;
y = y0;
print f (“\n\nX\t\tY\n”);
while (x < xn)
{
```

```
m1 = f (x0, y0);
m2 = f ((x0 + h/2.0),(y0 + m1 * h/2.0));
m3 = f ((x0 + h/2.0), (y0 + m2 * h/2.0));
m4 = f ((x0 + h), (y0 + m3 * h));
m = ((m1 + 2 * m2 + 2 * m3 + m4)/6);
y = y + m * h;
x = x + h;
print f ("%f \t %f \n," x, y);
}
getch ();
}
float f (float x, float y)
{
float m;
m = (x – y)/(x + y);
return m;
}
```

OUTPUT:

```
Enter x0, y0, xn, h:
X=
Y=
```

2. A polluted lake has an initial concentration of a bacteria of 107 parts/m^3. The concentration of the bacteria will reduce as fresh water enters the lake. Find the concentration of the pollutant after 7 weeks.

dc/dt + 0.06 c = 0

The differential equation that governs the concentration c of the pollution as a function of time (in week) is given by

dc/dt + 0.06 c = 0, c (0) = 10^6

dc/dt = – 0.06 c

f (t, c) = – 0.06 c

$c_{i+1} = c_I + 1/6 (k_1 + 2 k_2 + 2 k_3 + k_4) h$

For i = 0, t = 0, $c_0 = 10^7$

$k_1 = f (t_0, c_0)$

$= f (t_0, c_0)$

= f (0, 10^7)

= – 0.06 (10^7)

= – 60000

$k_2 = (t_0 + 1/2 \times h, c_0 + 1/2 k_1 h)$

$= f (0 + 1/2 + h, c_0 + 1/2 k_1 h)$

= f (0 + 1/ 2 x 3.5,107 + 1/ 2(- 600000)3.5)

= f (1.75,8950000)

= – 0.06(8950000)

$= -537000$
$= f(0 + 1/2 \times 3.5, 10\ 7 + 1/2 (-537000)\ 3.5)$
$= f(1.75, 9060300)$
$= f(-0.06 (9060300)$
$= -543620$
$k_4 = f(t_0 + h, c_0 + k_3 h)$
$= f(0 + 3.5, 10\ 7 + (-543620)\ 3.5)$
$= f(3.5, 8097300)$
$= -0.06 (8097300)$
$= -485840$
$c_1 = c_0 + (6/1\ k_1 + 2k_2 + 2k_3 + k_4)h$
$= 10\ 7 + 1/6 (-600000 + 2 (-53700) + 2 (-543620)$
$+ (-485840))\ 3.5$
$= 10\ 7 + 1/6 (-3247100)\ 3.5$
$= 8.1059 \times 10^6$ parts/m^3

c_1 is the approximate concentration of bacteria at
$T = t_1 = t_0 + h = 0 + 3.5 = 3.5$ parts/m^3
$C (3.5) = c_1 = 8.1059\times 10$ parts/m^3
For $i = 1$, $t_1 = 3.5$, $C_1 = 8.1059\times 10^6$
$k_1 = f(t_1, c_1)$
$= f(3.5, 8.1059 \times 10^6)$
$= -0.06 (8.1059 \times 10^6)$
$= -486350$
$k_2 = f(t_1 + 1/2 \times h, c_1 + 1/2\ k_1 h)$
$= f(3.5 + 1/2 \times 3.5, 8105900 + 1/2 (-486350)$
$3.5)$
$= f(5.25, 7254800)$
$= -0.06 (7254800)$
$= -435290)$
$k_3 = f(t_1 + 1/2 \times h, c_1 + 1/2\ k_2 h)$
$= f(3.5 + 1/2 \times 3.5, 8105900 + 1/2 (-440648)$
$3.5)$
$= f(5.25, 7344100)$
$= -0.06 (7444100)$
$= -440648$
$k_4 = f(t_1 + h, c_1 + k_3 h)$
$= f(3.5 + 3.5, 8105900 + (-440648)\ 3.5)$
$= f(7, 6563600)$
$= 0.06 (6563600)$
$= -393820$
$c_2 = c_1 + 1/6 (k_1 + 2\ k_2 + 2k_3 + k_4)\ h$
$= 8105900 + 1/6 + (-486350 + 2 \times (-435290) + 2$
$\times (-440648) + (-393820)) \times 3.5$
$= 8105900 + 1/6 (-2632000) \times 3.5$

= 6.5705×10^6 parts/m^3

c_2 is the approximate concentration of bacteria at $t_2 = t_1 + h = 3.5 + 3.5 = 7$ weeks c

$c(7) = c_2 = 6.5705 \times 10^6$ parts/m^3

PROGRAM:

```
#include <conio. h>
# include <iostream.h>
Void main ()
{
loat c[10], f, t[10], h, n;
cout << "Enter the initial values of concentration
of bacteria:";
int i;
cin >> c [0];
cout << "Enter the initial value of time:";
cin >> t [0]
cout << "Enter the value of time in weeks at
which we want to see the concentration:";
cin >> f;
cout << "Enter the difference: ";
cin >> h;
n = (f – c [0])/h;
for (i = 1; i < = n; i ++)
{
a = 0
k1 = – (.06 * c [a]);
k2 = – h *(.06 * (c [a] + k1/2));
k3 = – h * (.06* (c [a] + k2/2));
k4 = – h * (.06 * (c [a] + k3));
k = (k1 + 2 * k2 + 2 * k3 + k4)/6;
y [i] = y [a] + 1;
```

```
a++;
}
Cout <<"/n table";
For (i – 0; i < n: i++)
{
cout << " \ t x = %f \ t y = %f," val [i] [0], val [i]
[1];
cout << " \ n";
getch ();
}
```

Output:

Enter the initial values of concentration of bacteria:
Enter the initial value of time:
Enter the value of time in weeks at which we want to see the concentration:
Enter the difference:

7.5. NUMEROV'S METHOD

Numerov's method is also known as Cowell's method. Numerov's method is an implicit fourth order method in order to find out or determine the solution of the second order differential equation y"(x) = f (x, y) with initial conditions $y(x_0) = y_0$, $y'(x_0) = y'_0$.

Consider that the integrand f (x, y) does not rely on the value of y.'

Numerov's algorithm is derived with the help of summing the Taylor series approximations for y (x + h) and y (x – h), then substituting the value of f (x, y) for y" (x) and in the end, substituting the expression, as follows

$[f(x + h, y(x + h)) - 2 f(x, y) + f(x - h), y(x - h))]/h^2$

for the second derivative of f (x, y (x)) with respect to x. The result can be written as,

$y(x + h) + y(x - h) = 2 y(x) + h^2 f(x, y) + (h^2/12)(f(x + h, y(x + h)) - 2 f(x, y) + f(x - h, y(x - h)))$.

Let $x_n = x_0 + nh$, y_n be the approximation to $y(x_n)$, and $f_n = f(x_n, y_n)$, the Numerov's method proceeds recursively with the help of the implicit equation for y_{n+1} as follows:

$Y_{n+1} = 2y_n - y_n - 1 + h^2 (f_n + (f_{n+1} - 2 f_n + f_{n-1})/12)$.

To start the step of recursion, two consecutive starting values of y are needed. Out of which, one is y_0 and the second starting value is y_1 is approximated with the help of a Runge Kutta Method.

Particular classes of problems may have a more accurate estimate for y_1.

Richardson extrapolation may be used in order to elevate both the order as well as the accuracy.

7.5.1. Function List

void Numerovs_Method (double (*f)(double, double), double (*g)(double, double, double), double y[], double x0, double c, double h, int richardson_columns, int number_of_steps)

This function uses the Numerov's method in order to find out or determine the solution of the initial value problem, y" = f(x, y); y(x0) = y[0] and y'(x0) = c, at x0 + nh where for n =1, number_of_steps, and h is the step size.

The function g (x, h, u) returns the value y in such a way that u = y – h^2 f(x, y)/12. The argument max_columns is the number of step size halving + 1 used in Richardson extrapolation so that if richardson_columns = 1 then no extrapolation to the limit is performed.

On input, y[0] is the value of y(x) at x = x0. On output y[n] is the value of y(x) at x = x0 + n h for n =0, number_of_steps.

7.6. PARTIAL DIFFERENTIAL EQUATION

A PDE (which is a short form for Partial Differential Equation) is a mathematical equation. Partial Differential Equation is consisting of two independent variable or more than two independent variables, as unknown function (which is dependent on those variable), and the partial derivatives of the unknown function by the means of the independent variables.

The order of a PDE is the order to highest derivative involved with respect to that particular equation. By the means of a PDE, a solution (or a particular solution) is a function that solves the whole equation. In simple words, a solution changes the PDE into an identity when it is put into a particular equation.

A solution is known as general, if the solution is consisting of all particular solution of the equation concerned. The term "exact solution" is every so often used with respect to the second order non-linear PDE or higher order non-linear PDE, in order to specify a particular solution.

Partial differential equations are used to formulate with the help of mathematics, in this way, it provides assistance in order to find out the solution of, physical along with the other problems that consisting of functions of various variables. For example, propagation of heat or sound, flow of the fluid, elasticity, electrodynamics, electrostatics, and so on.

7.7. FIRST-ORDER PARTIAL DIFFERENTIAL EQUATIONS

7.7.1. General Form of First-Order Partial Differential Equation

A first-order PDE with 'n' independent variables has the general form (Figure 7.2).

$F(x_1, x_2, \ldots, x_n, w, \partial w/\partial x_1, \partial w/\partial x_2, \ldots, \partial w/\partial x_n)=0,$

In which, $w=w(x_1, x_2, \ldots, x_n)$ is the unknown function and F (...) is a given function.

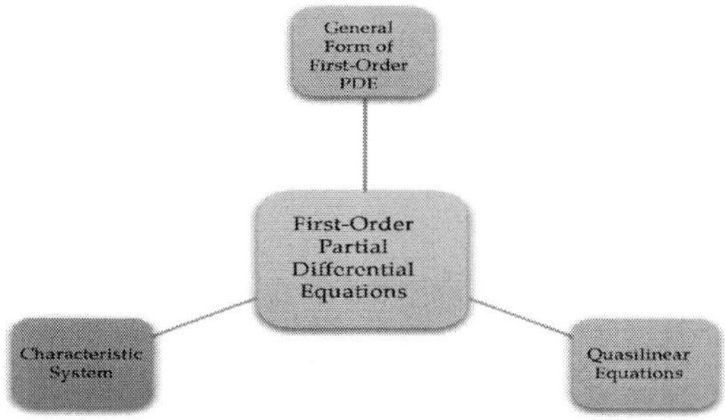

Figure 7.2. First order partial differential equations.

7.7.2. Quasilinear Equations

General form of first-order quasilinear Partial Differential Equation (PDE)

A first-order quasilinear PDE with two independent variables has the general form

$f(x,y,w)\partial w/\partial x+g(x,y,w)\partial w/\partial y=h(x, y,w)$. (1)

These sorts of equations are come across in several numbers of various applications (for instance, continuum mechanics, gas dynamics, hydrodynamics, heat, and mass transfer, wave theory, acoustics, multiphase flows, chemical engineering, and so on).

If the functions f, g, and h are independent of the unknown w, then equation number (1) is said to be linear.

7.7.3. Characteristic System: General Solution

The system of ODEs, as shown below

$dx/f(x,y,w)=dy/g(x,y,w)=dw/h(x,y,w)$ (2)

Is known as the characteristic system of equation number (1). Let's assume that two independent particular solutions of this system have been found in the form of:

$u_1(x,y,w)=C_1,u_2(x,y, w)=C_2$ (3)

In which, C_1 and C_2 are two arbitrary constants. These kinds of particular solutions are said to be the integrals of system (2). Then the general solution of equation number (1) can be written in the form of

$\Phi(u_1,u_2)=0,$ (4)

In which, Φ is an arbitrary function of two variables. With the help of equation number (4) solved for u_2, an individual or a person, every so often lay down the general solution in the form $u_2=\Psi(u_1)$, where $\Psi(u)$ is an arbitrary function of one variable.

Thing to consider in characteristic system, If $h(x,y,w)\equiv 0$, then $w=C_2$ can be used as the second integral in the equation number (3).

7.8. SECOND-ORDER PARTIAL DIFFERENTIAL EQUATIONS

Talking about second order linear PDE or PDE which is having two independent variables, is in the form of:

$$a(x,y)\ [\partial^2 w/\partial x^2] + 2b(x,y)\ [\partial^2 w/\partial x\partial y] + c(x,y)\ [\partial^2 w/\partial y^2] = \alpha(x,y)\ [\partial w/\partial x] + \beta(x,y)\ [\partial w/\partial y] + \gamma(x,y)w + \delta(x,y). \quad (1)$$

If $\delta\equiv 0$, in the equation number (1) is a homogeneous linear equation, and if $\delta\not\equiv 0$, it is a nonhomogeneous linear equation. Then the functions $a(x,y)$, $b(x,y)$., $\gamma(x,y)$, $\delta(x,y)$ are said to be the coefficients of equation number (1).

There are several numbers of characteristics of a homogeneous linear equation (with $\delta\equiv 0$), which are mentioned as follows:

A homogeneous linear equation has a particular solution $w = 0$.

The principle of linear superposition holds; namely, if $w_1(x, y)$, $w_2(x, y)$, $w_n(x, y)$ are the particular solutions of a homogeneous linear equation. In that case, the function $A_1 w_1(x, y) + A_2 w_2(x, y) + \cdots + A_n w_n(x, y)$, where A_1, A_2, A_n are the arbitrary numbers. And, in addition to this, is an exact solution with respect to that particular PDE. Let's assume that equation number (1) has a particular solution $\tilde{w} = \tilde{w}(x, y; \mu)$ which rely on a parameter, known as μ, and the coefficients of the linear differential equation are independent of μ (but can rely on x and y). In this case, with the help of differentiating $\tilde{w}$ with respect to that parameter, that is μ, an individual or a person can get other solutions to the equation, $\partial\tilde{w}/\partial\mu$, $\partial^2\tilde{w}/\partial\mu^2$, …, $\partial^k\tilde{w}/\partial\mu^k$,…

Let $\tilde{w} = \tilde{w}(x, y; \mu)$ be a particular solution as it is mentioned in property number 3. Multiplying $\tilde{w}$ with the help of an arbitrary function $\varphi(\mu)$ and integrating the consequential expression with respect to μ over some period of time, that is $[\mu_1, \mu_2]$, an individual or a person can get a new function $\int_{\mu_1}^{\mu_2}\tilde{w}(x, y; \mu)\,\varphi(\mu)\,d\mu$. And, that function is also a solution with respect to the original homogeneous linear equation. Let's assume that the coefficients of the homogeneous linear equation, in equation number (1) are independent of x.

In this case:

- there is a particular solution in the form of $w = e^{\lambda x} u(y)$, in which λ is an arbitrary number and u (y) can be find out with the help of a linear second-order ODE; and
- differentiating any particular solution with respect to x also results in a particular solution to equation number (1).

Among the properties that are mentioned above, properties 2 – 5 are extensively used in order to find out the solutions to problems that are governed by the linear Partial Differential Equations.

7.8.1. Semi Linear and Non-linear Second-Order Partial Differential Equations

A second-order semi linear PDE is consisting of two independent variables, and these variables are in the form of:

$$a(x,y)\,[\partial^2 w/\partial x^2] + 2b(x,y)\,[\partial^2 w/\partial x\partial y] + c(x,y)\,[\partial^2 w\partial y^2] = F(x,y,w,\partial w/\partial x,\partial w/\partial x).(2)$$

With respect to a general case, a second-order nonlinear PDE with two independent variables has the form of

$$F(x,y,w,\partial w/\partial x,\partial w/\partial y,\partial^2 w/\partial x^2,\partial^2 w/\partial x\partial y,\partial^2 w/\partial y^2)=0.$$

The classification as well as the procedure for decreasing the linear along with the semilinear equations of the form, like equation number (1) and equation number (2) to a canonical form are only find out with the help of the left-hand side of the equations.

7.9. CLASSIFICATION OF SECOND-ORDER PARTIAL DIFFERENTIAL EQUATIONS

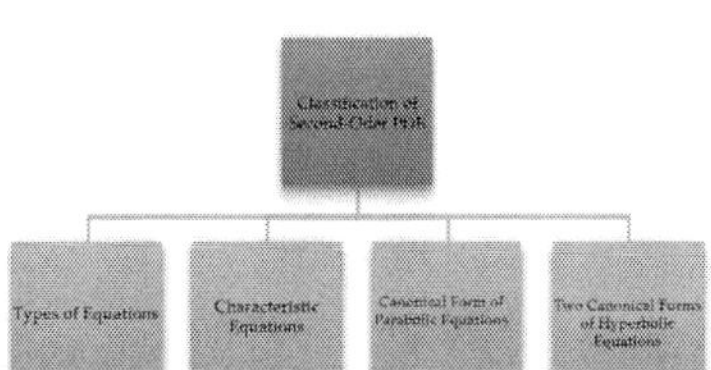

Figure 7.3. Classification of second order partial differential equation.

7.9.1. Types of Equations

Any kind of semi linear PDE which is of second order and having two independent variables, as shown in the equation number (2) can be reduced, with the help of a suitable manipulations, into a simple equation, which is having combination of one of the three highest derivatives.

Given a point (x,y), in the equation number (2) as mentioned above, is said to be

Parabolic if $b^2 - ac=0$;

Hyperbolic if $b^2-ac>0$,

Elliptic if $b^2-ac<0$.

at this particular setting.

7.9.2. Characteristic Equations

To reduce the equation number (2) in to a canonical form, an individual or a person should first write out the characteristic equation, which is:

$$a(dy)^2 - 2bdx.\, dy+c(dx)^2=0,$$

which with $a\neq0$ splits into two equations

$$a\, dy - (b + \sqrt{(b^2 - ac)})\, dx = 0 \qquad \text{(i)}$$

and

$$a\, dy - (b - \sqrt{(b^2 - ac)})\, dx = 0 \qquad \text{(ii)}$$

and then find out their general integrals.

Things to consider in the characteristic equation. If $a\equiv0$, the simpler equations

$$dx = 0,$$

$$2b\, dy - c\, dx = 0.$$

should be used instead of equation number (i) and equation number (ii). The first equation has the obvious general solution, which is x=C.

7.9.3. Canonical Form of Parabolic Equations (Case $b^2-ac=0$)

In the case of Canonical Form of Parabolic Equations, equations number (i) and equation number (ii) coincide and have a common general integral,

$$U(x,y)=C.$$

With the help of passing from x, y to new independent variables ξ, η with respect to the relations

$\xi=u(x,y)$,

$\eta=\eta(x,y)$,

in which, $\eta=\eta(x,y)$ is any twice differentiable function that fulfils the condition of a nondegeneracy of the Jacobian $D(\xi,\eta)/D(x,y)$ in the particular given domain, an individual or a person can reduce the equation number (2) in the form of a canonical equation, as mentioned below:

$$\partial^2 w/\partial\eta^2=F1(\xi,\eta,w,\partial w/\partial\xi,\partial w/\partial\eta). \quad \text{(iii)}$$

As η, one can take $\eta=x$ or $\eta=y$.

It is apparent that the transformed equation number (iii) has only one highest-derivative term.

7.9.4. Two Canonical Forms of Hyperbolic Equations (Caseb^2 – ac>0)

1. . The General Integrals

$u_1(x,y)=C_1$,

$u_2(x,y)=C_2$

The general integrals of the equations number (i) and the equation number (ii) are real and different as well. These integrals find out two different families of the real characteristics.

With the help of passing from x, y to new independent variables ξ, η with respect to the relations

$\xi=u_1(x,y)$,

$\eta=u_2(x,y)$,

an individual can reduce the equation number (2) in the form of

$$\partial^2 w/\partial\xi\partial\eta=F2(\xi,\eta,w,\partial w/\partial\xi,\partial w/\partial\eta).$$

This process or this step is known as the first canonical form of a hyperbolic equation.

2. The Transformation

$\xi=t+z$,

$\eta=t-z$

The transformation brings the equation, that is mentioned above in to the other canonical form,

$$\partial^2 w/\partial t^2 - \partial^2 w/\partial z^2 = F3(t,z,w,\partial w/\partial t,\partial w/\partial z),$$

In which, $F_3=4F_2$. This is known as the second canonical form of a hyperbolic equation.

7.10. CONCLUSION

In the conclusion of the chapter, there are several numbers of various methods are present in order to solve or find the approximate solution to any sort of ODEs such as Taylor series, Euler's Method, Runge Kutta Method, Numerov's method, and so on.

Taking about the PDEs, there are several numbers of various forms of it, such as first order PDEs, second order PDEs, third order PDEs, fourth order PDEs.

These different kinds of differential equation can be used, in order to find the approximate value of that particular equation. These several methods that are mentioned above in the chapter can also be applied in computer programming such as C, C++, and python as well.

REFERENCES

1. (n.d). *Euler's Method, Taylor Series Method, Runge Kutta Methods, Multi-Step Methods and Stability*. [ebook] pp. 1–6. Available at: http://www.cfm.brown.edu/people/sg/AM35odes.pdf (accessed on 4 June 2020).
2. (n.d). *Lecture 5: Taylor Series.* [ebook] Available at: https://math.okstate.edu/people/binegar/2233-S99/2233-l05.pdf (accessed on 4 June 2020).
3. Bourne, M., (2018). *11. Euler's Method-A Numerical Solution for Differential Equations*. [online] Intmath.com. Available at: https://www.intmath.com/differential-equations/11-eulers-method-des.php (accessed on 4 June 2020).
4. Cambridge University, (1992). *Chapter 16. Integration of Ordinary Differential Equations.* [ebook] NUMERICAL RECIPES IN C: THE ART OF SCIENTIFIC COMPUTING. Available at: http://tnt.phys.uniroma1.it/twiki/pub/TNTgroup/AngeloVulpiani/runge.pdf (accessed on 4 June 2020).
5. Christopher, A. B., (2017). *Numerical Methods for Solving Differential Equations.* [ebook] California, USA: Mathematics & Science Learning Center Computer Laboratory. Available at: http://calculuslab.deltacollege.edu/ODE/7-C-1/7-C-1-h-c.html (accessed on 4 June 2020).
6. Christopher, A. B., (2017). *Numerical Methods-Runge-Kutta Method.* [online] Calculuslab.deltacollege.edu. Available at: http://calculuslab.deltacollege.edu/ODE/7-C-3/7-C-3-h.html (accessed on 4 June 2020).
7. Duane, Q. N., (n.d). *An Introduction to Ordinary Differential Equations-Math Insight*. [online] Mathinsight.org. Available at: https://mathinsight.org/ordinary_differential_equation_introduction (accessed on 4 June 2020).
8. Fletcher, S., (2017). *Numerical Solutions to Initial Value Problems. Data Assimilation for the Geosciences,* [online] pp. 273–315. Available at: https://www.sciencedirect.com/science/article/pii/B9780128044445000088 (accessed on 4 June 2020).
9. Gowri, P., Priyadharsini, S., & Maheswari, T., (2017). *A Case Study on Runge Kutta 4th Order Differential Equations and its Application.* [online] researchgate.net. Available at: https://www.researchgate.net/publication/320124650_A_Case_Study_on_Runge_Kutta_4_th_

Order_Differential_Equations_and_Its_Application (accessed on 4 June 2020).

10. Michael. Z., (1998). *Runge-Kutta Methods*. [online] Web.mit.edu. Available at: http://web.mit.edu/10.001/Web/Course_Notes/Differential_Equations_Notes/node5.html (accessed on 4 June 2020).
11. Miletics, E., & Moln´arka, G., (n.d). *Taylor Series Method with Numerical Derivatives for Numerical Solution of ODE Initial Value Problems.* [ebook] Gy˝or: Department of Mathematics, Sz´echenyi Istvan University, Gy˝or. Available at: http://hej.sze.hu/ANM/ANM-030110-B/anm030110b.pdf (accessed on 4 June 2020).
12. My math lib, (n.d). *Numerov's Method.* [online] Mymathlib.com. Available at: http://www.mymathlib.com/diffeq/second_order/numerov.html (accessed on 4 June 2020).
13. Paul, D., (2018). *Differential Equations-Euler's Method.* [online] Tutorial.math.lamar.edu. Available at: http://tutorial.math.lamar.edu/Classes/DE/EulersMethod.aspx (accessed on 4 June 2020).
14. Polyanin, A., Schiesser, W., & Zhurov, A., (2008). *Partial Differential Equation.* Scholarpedia, [online] *3*(10), p. 4605. Available at: http://www.scholarpedia.org/article/Partial_differential_equation#Canonical_form_of_parabolic_equations_.28case_.5C.28b.5E2-ac.3D0.5C.29.29 (accessed on 4 June 2020).
15. Science direct, (2020). *Runge-Kutta Method: An Overview | Sciencedirect Topics.* [online] Sciencedirect.com. Available at: https://www.sciencedirect.com/topics/earth-and-planetary-sciences/runge-kutta-method (accessed on 4 June 2020).
16. Wave Fields in Real Media, (2015). *Numerical Methods*. [online] pp. 509–573. Available at: https://www.sciencedirect.com/science/article/pii/B9780080999999000091 (accessed on 4 June 2020).

CHAPTER

8

APPROXIMATE DYNAMIC PROGRAMMING

CONTENTS

Approximate Dynamic Programming is one of the most essential process of solving the issues related to time control forms that is the complex Markov Decision Process. Here, in this chapter, different aspects of the approximate dynamic programming have been described. Initially, the issues related to the algorithms of the approximate dynamic programming have been provided. Models of the reinforcement learning have been evaluated in this chapter. Reinforcement learning is described in this chapter since it is an important part of machine learning and computer science field.

This chapter also helps to evaluate the challenges of the dynamic programming. Linear programming approach has been described in relation to the approximate dynamic programming. At the end of the chapter high dimensional resource allocation issues have been dealt with.

8.1. INTRODUCTION

In order to resolve mathematical problems in terms of approximate dynamic programming (ADP) numerical analysis is considered, which is a branch of computer science that develops and implement the required algorithm for the problem.

The main focus of numerical methods is usually on the implementation of the numerical algorithms. Therefore, to provide systematic techniques for solving mathematical problems numerically is the main aim of these methods.

> Modern digital computers are very fast and efficient in performing arithmetic operations and with help of these computers numerical methods solve the mathematical problems, as numerical methods are well suited for it.

It is said that, generally it is required that it should be started from an initial data for the process of solving problems using high precision digital computers. So, to produce the required results the concerned appropriate algorithms are then executed.

Approximate digital programming are the methods which are used on the numerical data. Hence, by the errors in the data, or the errors in the method, or both the error in the computed result may be produced.

While discussing ADP in the computer science and machine learning community, the term reinforcement learning is often used. Wide range of solid results are associated with this term, which obtained both analytically and empirically by considering learning in the arena of Markov decision processes (MDPs).

Learning results assume discrete cases in most of its analyses and applications, reinforcement, where the state and action spaces can be enumerated and stored in memory. Over the time the performance of the system can be improved through interactions with the environment and through past experience.

And there is some another class of systems, adaptive critic designs, address some very similar issues, namely, to develop learning systems. Calculus of variations which is used in optimal control theory is the foundation of this approach on which it is built.

Designing of learning system is introduced possibly by the problem construct of adaptive critic designs that can handle continuous state space problems or the possibility of addressing generalization issues and design robustness issues.

Direct neural dynamic programming (direct NDP) is introduced in this chapter. The term "direct" is influenced by the adaptive control literature where "direct adaptive control" means no plant model, and thus to find appropriate and convergent control laws and control parameters no plant parameter estimation takes place, but instead certain plant information is used directly.

In direct NDP, to represent both the value function (for control performance evaluation) and the action function (for control law generation) two generic (neural) function approximates are used.

Moreover, it is said that in learning the control the state information is used directly where the controller parameters are the weight parameters in the action function implemented by a neural network.

Therefore, to action-dependent heuristic programming direct NDP is a model-independent approach which is considered.

Several important ideas and implementations of model-based approximate dynamic programming (ADP) including heuristic dynamic programming (HDP), dual heuristic dynamic programming (DHP), and globalized dual heuristic dynamic programming (GDHP) is the class of adaptive critic designs which is encompasses.So, there is completely different feature of the adaptive critic designs is that it is having the potential of addressing large scale problems, and along with this continuous state and control problems. To demonstrate the feasibility of some key adaptive critic design techniques several applications and case studies have been developed where in the family as a nonlinear controller globalized dual dynamic programming has been found the most effective.

It is said that direct NDP is expected to achieve computational efficiency and reliability due to its simple, completely gradient driven implementation in addressing large scale problems, as a model-independent approach to the action-dependent HDP.

8.2. APPROXIMATE DYNAMIC PROGRAMMING

A powerful set of strategies for problems that are hard is offered by ADP because they are large, but this is not the only application.

Sometimes small problems are also considered as the hard problem because there is lack of use of the formal model of the information process, or the transition function is not known. For example, there is mathematical model that describes the changes in prices in an asset. So, in this case, it is not possible to compute the expectation.

On the other hand, how the economy of a small country responds to loans is the problem of modeling which should be considered from the International Monetary Fund. So how the economy responds to the size of a loan, if it is not known by anyone, then this means that transition function is not known.

So, moving forward through states is does not means that it will solve the problem of high-dimensional state spaces or updating estimates of the value of being in only the states that any one has visit.

Instead, with the statistical problem of estimating the value of being in each state it replaces the computational burden of looping over every state. So, there is general rule which states that it should already be known to the concerned person that which states need to be evaluated and it is not necessary that to have the value of being in every state (Figure 8.1).

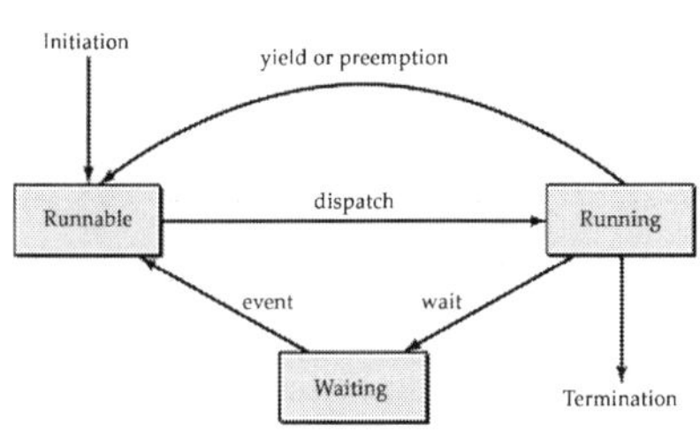

Figure 8.1. Scheduling in approximate dynamic programming.

Source: Image by Gitlab.

However, it is said that to exploit the structure of the problem there are a number of strategies which can be use, as in reality which does not really allow to do is something that backward dynamic programming.

As with the use of these methods an experience will be gained and after the experience it will be observed that some understanding of the structure of the problem tends to be critical. The value function approximation $\bar{V}$ as a kind of policy is useful to think.

Typically, it has been observed that there will be an option of choosing between different classes of functional approximations, for example, functions that are linear in the state variable, separable quadratic, nonseparable, and so on.

So as being a class of policies the thought can be given to each class of functions. It is said that finding the best set of parameters is considered equivalent to the choosing the best policy within a class.

As if transition is made to high dimensional decision vectors, then the applications will be encounter where the myopic problem (that is, the problem of maximizing the one-period reward) is itself fairly hard. In the management of physical assets where the myopic problem falls in one of the classes of hard optimization problems these situations typically arise.

8.2.1. Representations of Value Functions

A discrete representation of the value function is assumed by the classical dynamic programming. It means that it is required to estimate a parameter vs that gives the value of being in state, s for every state, $s \in S$.

The loop which is required in the backward dynamic programming is eliminated by the forward dynamic programming over all states, but it does not solve the classic "curse of dimensionality" in the state space.Forward dynamic programming is that having the main focus on the states that an individual or a person actually visit, but it also requires that having some idea of the value of being in a state that an individual might visit (this estimate is required to conclude that the state should not be visited).

In ADP there are every large-scale problem, and how to approximate the value function with a smaller number of parameters is the main focus to determine.On the other hand, in backward discrete dynamic programming, there is only one parameter per state, and it is said that to avoid searching over a large number of states. In forward dynamic programming, the major issue is statistical error as everyone is depending on Monte Carlo sampling.

8.2.2. Algorithmic Issues

There are two algorithmic challenges which are involved by the design of an approximation strategy. First, the surety is required that the value function approximation does not unnecessarily complicate the solution of the myopic problem.So, it has been assumed that myopic problem is solvable in a reasonable period of time. It is usually impossible to consider a value function that is of the discrete, table-lookup variety, if myopic problem is a linear or nonlinear program.

It is not required to introduce a potentially non concave value function, if myopic problem is continuously differentiable and concave. By contrast, if the myopic problem is considered as the discrete scheduling problem that is being solved with a search heuristic, then table-lookup value functions can work just fine.

An updating strategy should be advised when it is decided that on the structure of functional approximation. Classical statistical techniques are used to update statistical models, which are generally considered as the value functions.

Thus, while updating algorithm is in a recursive form it is very convenient. It is said that there is a strategy which will be too expensive for many of the applications because it fits a set of parameters by using a sequence of observations using standard regression techniques.

8.3. CHALLENGES OF DYNAMIC PROGRAMMING

In many of the settings the optimization of problems over time arises, which is ranging from the control of heating systems to managing entire economies. There are some examples including landing aircraft, purchasing new equipment, managing fleets of vehicles, selling assets, investing money in portfolios or just playing a game of tic-tac-toe or backgammon.

As if the above-mentioned problems will be encountered by different fields, than they tended to discover that certain fundamental equations described their behavior. As it is considered as the "optimality equations," different fields have rediscovered them by under names like dynamic programming and optimal control.

In operation research these topics are arise and this is also the main focus of this book. Some form of asset management can be categorized, with the understanding that this term refers to both physical and financial assets.

There is an important difference which is made between the problems that involve a single asset and those that involve multiple assets or asset classes. So, the problems which are associated with a single asset is ranging from selling a bond to routing a single aircraft, but also include playing a game of tic-tac-toe or planning an academic schedule to maximize the chances of graduating from college.

Landing an aircraft or controlling a robot could also be considered as the single-asset problems, but these examples are primarily exempted because of their emphasis on low-dimensional controls of continuously differentiable function.

Although important class of applications is represented by the single-asset problems, the book is continuously focusing on the problems that involve the management of multiple assets.

A mathematical framework for modeling problems where information and decisions evolve over time is represented where all of these problems can be formulated as dynamic programs.

Dynamic programming is a genuinely experienced part of applied arithmetic, yet it has engaged with the progress from hypothesis to calculation. The greater part of the reading material on unique programming center around issues where all the amounts are discrete.

An assortment of calculations exists for these issues; however, they regularly experience the ill effects of what is ordinarily referred to as the "curse of dimensionality" which has been discussed in the chapter.

Dynamic programming has its underlying foundations in a few fields. Designing and financial aspects will in general spotlight on issues with continuous states and choices, these networks refer to choices as controls, while the fields of tasks inquire about and artificial intelligence (AI) work basically with discrete states and choices (or activities).

Issues that are displayed with constant states and choices (and ordinarily in consistent time) are commonly tended to fall under the umbrella of "control hypothesis" though issues with discrete states and choices, demonstrated in discrete time, are learned finally under the umbrella of "Markov choice procedures."

Both of these subfields set up recursive conditions that rely upon the utilization of a state variable to catch history in a reduced manner.

The investigation of advantage the executive's issues (or all the more extensively, "asset assignment") is ruled by the field of numerical programming (or stochastic programming when it is supposed to expressly catch vulnerability), which has developed without relying upon the build of a state variable. The treatment draws vigorously from each of the three fields.

8.4. DYNAMIC PROGRAMMING DIALECTS

Sequential decision process give rise to the dynamic programming. There are a wide range of applications where the dynamic programming is applied. While the intentions were not to take anything from fundamental contribution of Bellman, the optimality conditions are to some degree self-evident.

Thus, they were found freely by the various networks wherein these issues emerge. The issues emerge in an assortment of engineering issues, commonly in constant time with continuous control parameters.

These applications offered to what is presently introduced as control hypothesis. While vulnerability is a significant issue in these issues, the details will in general spotlight on deterministic issues, the vulnerability is ordinarily in the estimation of the state or the parameters that oversee the framework (Figure 8.2).

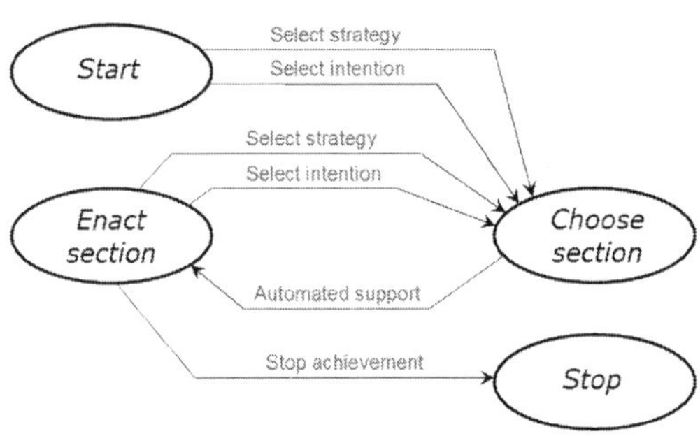

Figure 8.2. Meta process modeling.

Source: Image by Wikipedia.

Financial analysts embraced control hypothesis for an assortment of issues including the control of exercises from designating single spending plans or overseeing whole economies, truly at a shortsighted level.

Activities examine did the most to push the hypothesis of controlling stochastic issues, in this manner delivering the rich hypothesis of Markov choice procedures. Computer scientists, particularly those working in the domain of AI, found that dynamic writing computer programs was a helpful system for moving toward specific classes of AI issues known as reinforcement learning.It isn't just the situation that various networks found the basics of dynamic programming freely. They additionally found the computational difficulties that emerge in their answer, the "scourge of dimensionality."

As anyone might expect, various networks likewise autonomously found classes of arrangement calculations. As various networks found similar ideas and calculations, they created their personal vocabularies to go with them.

Thus, it can be understood that the Bellman conditions, the Hamiltonian, the Jacobian, the Hamilton-Jacobian, or the generally useful Hamilton-Jacobian-Bellman conditions (normally specified to as the HJB conditions).

Here, the expression "optimality conditions" is liked. There is a considerably more vocabularies for the sorts of calculations that are the point of convergence. Everybody has found that the regressive recursions required to tackle the optimality conditions don't fill in as the quantity of measurements enhance.

A lot of authors have autonomously found that an option is to step forward through time, utilizing iterative calculations to help gauge the worth capacity. This general procedure has been alluded to as forward dynamic programming, iterative dynamic programming, versatile dynamic programming, and neuro-dynamic programming.

In any case, the term that seems to have been most generally embraced is ADP. In some of the cases, the authors would find the calculations and just later find their relationship to old style dynamic programming.

The utilization of iterative calculations that are the premise of most ADP methodology, similarly, have their foundations in a field known as stochastic approximation techniques.

8.5. PROBLEMS OF COMPLEX RESOURCE ALLOCATION

There are numerous complex resource allocation (CRA) issues that can profit by ADP. These issues may include overseeing vehicle fleets (trucks, cars, airplane, trains).

It also include dispersing items through inventory chains, overseeing individuals in the military, what number of volunteers ought to be allocated to a specific kind of training, what number of individuals ought to be assigned to a specific base, and overseeing stores of wares, vitality products, for example, oil or coal, horticultural commodities, for example, corn or wheat.

For these issues, it is required to be decided not just how to manage an asset like where should the truck be sent, what preparing should the military enroll get, when should the producing plant be turned off, etc. (Figure 8.3).

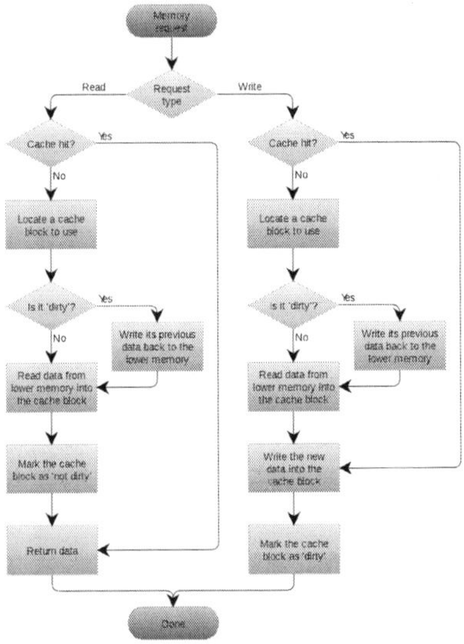

Figure 8.3. Cache computing in complex resource allocation.

Source: Image by Wikipedia.

Would it be advisable to move 10 or 20 trucks into an area? Would it be advisable to prepare 20 or 200 enlisted people to fix helicopters? Would it be advisable to buy 10 million or 20 million barrels of oil? These issues can be seen as dealing with an asset vector $R_t = (R_t a)a \in A$ where $R_t a$ is the amount of assets with characteristic a_n at time t.

For some issues, R_t comprises the state variable, and the strategies that have been presented in this part would concentrate on evaluating the worth $V_t(R_t)$ of being in state R_t. In any case, it is the situation that it is helpful to concentrate on the outlying estimation of $V_t(R_t)$ concerning R_t.

In order to explain, think about the issue of moving items (farming, coal, oil) from the purpose of creation through different intermediate storage facilities. Items might be offered to intermediate wholesalers or drew nearer to the last market.

Additionally, to the standard documentation, let $D_t a$ be the arbitrary interest for products of type a_n at time t, and $P_t a$ be the irregular cost. At time t, R_{t-1}, a unit of result of type a subsequent from choices (and data) from time t−1 is available with which to fulfill the interest in period t (recall: t is ordering the data content, not the accessibility of the item.

This algorithmic procedure, where a solitary huge issue has been isolated into a progression of little sub problems partitioned over existence, time moves left to right. In each sub problem are a progression of shaded boxes.

The containers in the left section represent various kinds of assets, and the crates on the privilege represent various sorts of requests. Anytime, it is required to illuminate what is referred to in straight programming as a transportation issue including the task of assets to requests.

However, choices at time t need to represent the estimation of assets later on. Rather than utilizing the estimation of the state later on, it utilizes the negligible estimation of extra assets later on. Utilizing ADP with a direct worth capacity guess includes relegating assets to requests at a given point in time, utilizing a worth capacity estimate of things to come.

Settling on choices and venturing forward, viably reproducing the way toward settling on choices and displaying the material science of the issue.

A regressive pass, where it locates the negligible estimation of assets later on, and step in reverse in time, figuring the minimal incentive at each subproblem as it steps forward.

This "backward pass" creates the peripheral worth v_t of assets of type a_n at each point in time. These are then smoothed to create an approximation that is updated.

8.5.1. Initialization Problem

The entirety of the techniques relies upon setting an underlying assessment $\bar{V}_0$ for the value function approximation. The introduction of the value function did not influence the capacity to locate the ideal arrangement; it just influenced the pace of combination.

In ADP, it is regularly the situation that the worth capacity estimation $\bar{V}_{n-1}$ utilized in emphasis on influences the decision of the activity taken and along these lines the following state visited.

The issue is for the traveling trucker. Here, the trucker relies upon the gauge of the estimation of being in a "state." If it is instated that the value function to a low worth, it will rapidly get higher appraisals for the states that it visits, which energizes choices that permit it to come back to these states.In the event that the underlying evaluations are excessively high, the procedure will support choices that take it to states that it has visited the least, since these will in general be the most elevated.

In the event that the state space (characteristic space) isn't excessively enormous, it will acquire the best answer utilizing a high initial estimate. In any case, if the state space and activity spaces are extremely large, it will unendingly investigate the states that it had never visited.

8.5.2. Sampling Strategies

There are two methodologies for testing states in ADP. Up to now, nonconcurrent ADP has been utilized, which infers that it just examples the states that is visited from the choice delivered by utilizing the approximate worth capacity.

A substitute procedure is synchronous ADP, where all states are tested at each emphasis. It is rapidly perceived that one cannot circle over all the states for issues with enormous state spaces. In the event that one could do this, one could utilize traditional in reverse dynamic programming.

There are, in any case, two employments of synchronous ADP. The first emerges in quite a while where one does not have a numerical model of the basic data process, and depend, rather, on the capacity to test the forward direction from an exogenous source.

For such issues, one can't process the desire for the worth capacity later on and need to rely upon tests from an exogenous source. The subsequent use is spurred by hypothetical issues.

Assembly proofs are accessible for table-query adaptations of synchronous calculations, where one can misuse the presumption that all states are visited boundlessly regularly. These necessities are not fulfilled when one utilizes offbeat calculations.

8.6. DYNAMIC PROGRAMMING WITH MISSING OR INCOMPLETE MODELS

Some physical frameworks are complex to such an extent that one can't portray them with scientific models, however, one can watch practices straightforwardly.

In the reinforcement learning network (RLN), these are now referred to as immediate models; taking care of issues without an unequivocal model is alluded to as sans model dynamic programming. There are three key numerical models utilized in dynamic programming (Figure 8.4).

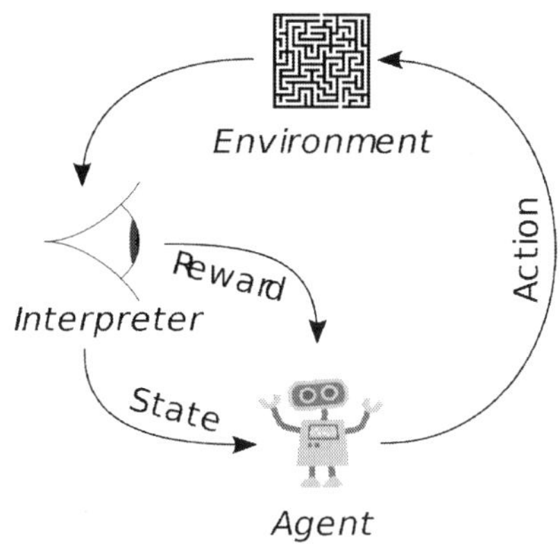

Figure 8.4. Example of reinforcement learning.

Source: Image by Wikimedia.

The first is a model of the exogenous data process. If one is examining a procedure where the arbitrariness represents the Poisson appearance of requests at a rate that is anything but difficult to gauge, at that point it isn't difficult to develop a numerical model of the interest procedure.

In the event that the issue is the displaying of financing costs of various nations, one face an issue with complex connections between loan fee streams, and across time. The second kind of model is the change work, which determines which state one progress to given a state, activity, and data.It is conceivable that regardless of whether one could gauge the state where one knows both the activity and the data, one despite everything probably won't know precisely what state one will land. Sometimes, one can approximate the change capacity and view errors between what one expected to occur and what really occurs as essentially missing data on the state variable.

However, as the model shows, the fundamental model may not be precise, which restrains the capacity to test arrangements, for example, expanding the quantity of hours a driver can move in a day. The third model is simply the choice capacity.

We think one are catching all the significant commitments and requirements in the goal work, yet this is basically not continually going to be the situation. There are various models where a human administrator will settle on choices dependent on data not accessible to the model.

Such outside direction is known as a boss and preparing an approximate dynamic program within the sight of such a wellspring of data is known as supervisory learning. The expression "model free" is frequently used to imply that one doesn't have a one-advance progress framework, however, where one may have a change work.

This implies what one is missing is a model of the data procedure. For instance, one may not know the arrangement of results, or the likelihood of a result. This is run of the mill of information that is originating from a physical procedure.Such issues may have little state spaces, permitting us to utilize calculations that require examining all the states at each emphasis. Tackling issues along these lines is by and large alluded to as without model ADP.

8.7. MODELING DYNAMIC PROGRAMS

Great displaying starts with great documentation. Complex issues in resource the executives require significant control in documentation, since they consolidate the complexities of the first physical issue and to the test of displaying successive data and choice procedures.

Students will commonly see the demonstrating of time as especially unpretentious. Notwithstanding a longing to show issues precisely, one additionally should have the option to comprehend the structure of the issue, which can get lost in an ocean of complex documentation.

It is regular in course readings on dynamic programming to rapidly receive a standard view so the introduction can concentrate on dynamic programming standards and properties. The attention is on demonstrating and calculation, and the objective is to comprehend enormous scope, complex issues.

Therefore, one dedicates more consideration regarding demonstrating than would be found in other dynamic programming writings. The decision of documentation needs to offset recorded examples with the requirements of a specific issue class.

Documentation is simpler to learn in the event that it is memory helper (the letters appear as though what they mean) and minimized (keeping away from a bounty of images). Documentation additionally assists with connecting networks.For instance, it is basic in dynamic programming to allude to activities utilizing "a" (where an is discrete); in control hypothesis a choice (control) is "u" (which might be continuous).

For high dimensional issues, it is fundamental to draw on the field of scientific programming, where choices are ordinarily composed as "x" and asset imperatives are written in the standard structure Ax = b.

In this content, a significant number of issues include overseeing resources (assets) where one is attempting to amplify or limit a target subject to imperatives. Thus, one receives, however, much as could be expected, the documentation of math programming to assist us with crossing over the fields of math programming and dynamic programming.

Legitimate documentation is additionally basic for facilitating the change from basic illustrative issues to the kinds of certifiable issues that can emerge by and by.In tasks inquire about, it is entirely expected to allude to an advantage class (in account, it could be a currency advertise support, land or a stock; in the physical world, it could be a kind of airplane or train) as a "product" which may be filed as k in a lot of classes K.

In any case, as tasks advance, these benefit classes may get new measurements. A typical resource the board issue in railways is the development of freight cars, where there is an away from of various car types make up the "products."Real train units, be that as it may, have different properties, for example, who possesses them (supposed "pools"), the exact arrangement of the car, they shift in viewpoints, for example, the specific area of the entryway and locking system, for instance, their support status, and their tidiness. As these ascribes are added to the issue, the quantity of freight car types develops drastically.

8.7.1. Modeling Time

A study of the writing uncovers various styles toward demonstrating time. When utilizing discrete time, a few authors start at one while others start at zero. When tackling limited skyline issues, it is well known to record time by the quantity of time spans remaining, instead of passed time.

A few authors list a variable, state S_t, just like an element of data up through t-1, while others accept it incorporates data up through time t. t might be utilized to represent when a physical occasion really occurs, or when one first thinks about a physical occasion.

The disarray over demonstrating time emerges in huge part in light of the fact that there are two procedures that one need to catch: the progression of data, and the progression of physical and budgetary resources.

There are numerous uses of dynamic programming to deterministic issues where the progression of data doesn't exist. Essentially, there are numerous models where the appearance of the data about a physical resource, and when the data takes influence in the physical framework, are the equivalent.

For instance, the time at which a client genuinely shows up to a line is regularly demonstrated, just like equivalent to when the data about the client initially shows up. Correspondingly, one frequently accepts that one can sell a benefit at a market cost when the cost gets known.

However, there is a rich assortment of issues where the data procedure and physical procedure are unique. A purchaser may buy an alternative now (a data occasion) to purchase an item later on (the physical occasion).

Clients may call an aircraft (the data event) to fly on a future flight (the physical event). An electric force organization needs to buy hardware currently to be utilized a couple of years later. These issues represent instances of slacked data procedures and power to expressly show the instructive and physical events.

8.7.2. Modeling Assets

A considerable lot of the models in this book are of genuinely complex issues, yet one commonly starts with generally straightforward issues. one need documentation that permits us to advance from easy to complex issues in a characteristic manner.

The principal issue one manages is the test of demonstrating single and various resources. In designing, a famous issue is to utilize dynamic programming to decide how to best set down an airplane, or control a force producing plant.

In software engineering, scientists in computerized reasoning should utilize a computer to play a round of backgammon or chess. one would allude to these applications as single resource issues. The "framework" would be the airplane, and the state variable would portray the position, speed, and increasing speed of the airplane.

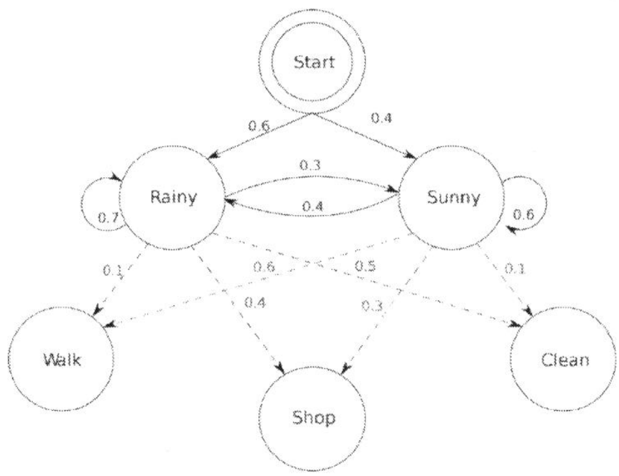

Figure 8.5. Hidden Markov model.

Source: Image by Wikipedia.

If one somehow happened to show the issue of flying a solitary airplane as a dynamic program, one would have significant trouble stretching out this model to all the while deal with various airplane.

The differentiation between demonstrating a solitary resource, (for example, an airplane) and numerous benefits (dealing with an armada of airplane) is significant. Hence, one embrace uncommon documentation when one is demonstrating a solitary resource.

For instance, it is very regular when displaying a dynamic program to utilize a variable, for example, St to represent the "state" of the framework, where S_t could be the traits portraying a solitary airplane, or all the characteristics of an armada of airplane.

Unfortunately, utilizing such broad documentation camouflages the structure of the issue and altogether muddles the test of planning compelling computational calculations.

The trait at can be a solitary component or a vector, yet one will consistently accept that the vector isn't too huge (close to 10 or 20 components). On account of the briefest way issue, at would be the group number comparing to the crossing point where a driver needed to settle on a choice.

In the event that one is taking care of a benefit selling issue, at might catch whether the advantage has been sold, and potentially to what extent one has held it. For an undergrad arranging her course of study, at would be a vector portraying the quantity of courses she has taken to satisfy every necessity.

There is a huge range of issues that including displaying what one would call a solitary resource. In the event that there is no enthusiasm for stretching out the model to deal with different resources, at that point it might be increasingly normal to utilize St as the state variable.

8.7.2.1. State-Dependent Information Processes

The standard dynamic programming models necessitate that the circulation of the procedure pushing ahead be a component of the condition of the framework. This is a broader model than one with autonomous augmentations.

Strikingly, numerous models of Markov choice process use data forms that do, truth be told, show free additions. For instance, one may have a queuing issue where the condition of the framework is the quantity of clients in the line.

The quantity of appearances might be Poisson, and the quantity of clients served in an augmentation of time is resolved basically by the length of the line. It is conceivable, nonetheless, that the appearance procedure is a component of the length of the line itself.

State-subordinate data forms are increasingly hard to demonstrate and present extra parameters that must be assessed. In any case, from the viewpoint of dynamic programming, they don't present any essential complexities.For whatever length of time that the dissemination of results is reliant absolutely on the condition of the framework, one can apply the standard models. A probabilistic model would demand this is as yet the case with the driver; the way that the driver doesn't have the foggiest idea about the travel times on all the connections is just an issue of demonstrating the data the driver employments.

However, most designing students will think that its progressively characteristic to think about the data as relying upon the state.

8.8. LINEAR PROGRAMMING APPROACH TO ADP

Dynamic programming offers a way to deal with taking care of issues of stochastic control. Vital to the technique is the expense to go work, which is acquired by means of helpful Bellman's condition.

The area of the expense to-go work is the state space of the framework to be controlled, and dynamic programming calculations register and store a table comprising of one expense to-go esteem per state.

Unfortunately, the size of a state space ordinarily develops exponentially in the quantity of state factors. Known as the scourge of dimensionality, this wonder renders dynamic programming obstinate notwithstanding issues of down to earth scale.

Throughout the years, enthusiasm for ADP has been fueled to a huge degree by accounts of experimental achievement in applications, for example, backgammon, work shop booking, lift planning and valuing of American choices.

These contextual analyses point to ADP as a possibly useful asset for huge scope stochastic control. However, huge experimentation is engaged with most examples of overcoming adversity found in the writing, and duplication of a similar accomplishment in different applications has demonstrated troublesome.

This is somewhat because of a generally poor comprehension of how, why, and when ADP calculations work, and represents an obstruction to the utilization of such calculations in industry.

Consequently, the examination of execution and mistakes related with ADP calculations isn't just a fascinating hypothetical test yet in addition a pragmatic need, and the ongoing progressions in the hypothetical investigation of approximate direct programming can be seen as steps toward a definitive objective of forming ADP into a really commonsense, smoothed out system for supporting dynamic in enormous scope issues.

The form of approximate direct programming portrayed here and represents a variation of the calculation initially proposed by Schweitzer and Seidman. While the first ALP calculation may display poor scaling properties, the variant appreciates solid hypothetical certifications.

A focal inquiry regarding any ADP calculation is the way well it approximates the expense to-go work.

The nature of the estimate relies upon the decision of premise capacities, henceforth the mistake actuated by an ADP calculation is typically portrayed in relative terms one look at it against the best blunder that can be accomplished given the determination of premise capacities.

It presents a blunder bound building up that approximate direct programming yields an estimation mistake that is equivalent to as well as can be expected be accomplished given the choice of premise capacities.

Other than offering ensures about the conduct of the calculation, the bound gives understanding about the effect of the calculation's free parameters onto the last estimation, in this manner prompting some direction in their determination.

It likewise gives data about how well the calculation scales as the issue measurements increment. Examination of approximations to the expense to-go work include the decision of a measurement on the space of capacities over the state space that decides how great various approximations are seen to be.

Obviously, a definitive examination is the normal expense of the strategy incited by the estimation, and this ought to be reflected in the measurement being picked. It additionally remembers a headed for the normal cost increment because of utilizing arrangements created by approximate direct programming rather than the ideal strategy.

The bound proposes a characteristic measurement for correlation of various approximations to the expense to-go capacity and gives consolation that the estimate mistake limits viable are important, as they are expressed as far as a metric that is perfect with the common execution-based measurement.

The exhibition bound likewise gives direction on the best way to set the free parameters in the approximate linear programming (ALP) calculation in order to be in a way that advances the execution of the strategy being obtained.

8.8.1. Approximate Linear Programming

A great part of the exertion in the writing on approximate straight programming has been coordinated toward effective usage of the calculation. Some broad examination of the calculation can be found.

Trick and Zin, create heuristics for consolidating the straight programming approach with progressive state collection in two-dimensional issues. A portion of their lattice age methods depend on fixed state disseminations, which likewise show up in the investigation of state relevance loads introduced here.

A significant component of the direct programming approach is that it produces lower limits as approximations to the expense to-go work; Gordon talks about issues that may emerge from this reality and proposes limitation slowed down heuristics.

One of these issues is that the direct program utilized in the approximate straight programming calculation might be excessively compelled, which may prompt poor approximations or even infeasibility (Figure 8.6).

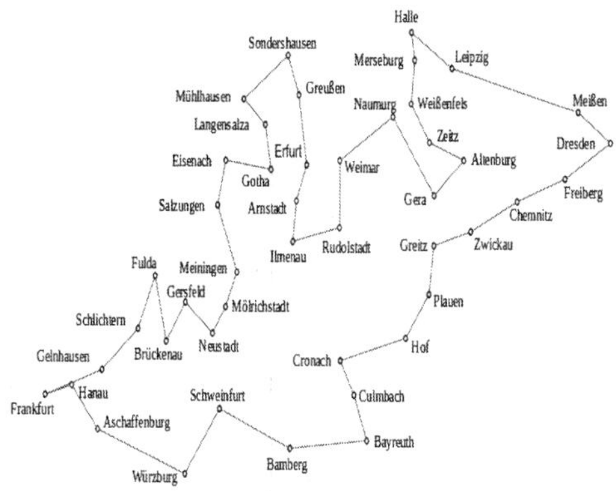

Figure 8.6. Traveling salesman problem in the approximate linear programming.

Source: Image by Wikipedia.

The methodology taken here forestalls this some portion of the distinctiveness between the variation of approximate direct programming introduced here and the first one proposed by Schweitzer and Seidmann is that the previous includes certain premise capacities that ensure possibility and furthermore lead to ensured limits on the guess blunder.

The requirement examining plan introduced here doesn't misuse any conceivable consistency related with structure in the limitations emerging in explicit issues, or a specific decision of premise capacities, which may prompt a lot more tightly limits or even strategies for accurate arrangement of the approximate LP.

Consequences of this nature can be found in the writing. Morrison and Kumar plan ALP calculations for queueing issues with a specific decision of premise works that renders everything except a generally modest number of requirements excess.

Guestrin et al. exploits the structure emerging when calculated direct designs are utilized for approximating the expense to-go work in figured MDP's to productively actualize ALP with a tractable number of requirements.

Conventional techniques intended to manage straight projects with enormous quantities of imperatives, for example, cutting planes and segment age, may likewise be helpful in explicit settings.

Schuurmans and Patrascu devise an imperative age conspire for considered MDP's with calculated straight structures that comes up short on the certifications of the calculation introduced, however, requires a little measure of time all things considered.

Grotschel presents a proficient cutting-plane strategy for the voyaging sales rep issue. Approximate direct programming additionally shows up in the writing as an instrument for investigation and arrangement of stochastic control issues in different application regions.

Paschalidis and Tsitsiklis apply the calculation to two-dimensional issues emerging in valuing of system administrations. Morrison and Kumar utilize approximate direct programming to determine limits on the exhibition of queueing systems.

Adelman utilizes ALP as an explanatory device supporting in the advancement of strategies for stock control. De Farias et al. utilize ALP to determine approaches for ideal asset designation in web server ranches.

8.9. ADP FOR HIGH-DIMENSIONAL RESOURCE ALLOCATION PROBLEMS

The distribution of human and physical assets over time is a principal issue that is fundamental to the management science.

For instance, a cargo transportation organization must oversee work force and gear to move shipments in a convenient way within the sight of an assortment of dynamic data forms: client requests, hardware failures, climate postponements, and disappointments of execution.

This is a high-dimensional issue since it includes countless assets, every one of which must be followed as it is influenced by choices and vulnerabilities. On a basic level, issues of dynamic asset allotment can be treated as Markov choice procedures and measured utilizing dynamic programming calculations.

Textbook dynamic programming calculations, for example, esteem emphasis and strategy cycle regularly require register time and memory that develop exponentially in the quantity of state factors, the quantity of choice factors, and the quantity of irregular factors that influence the framework in each time span. These three "curse of dimensionality" render such calculations infeasible for issues of pragmatic scale.

The calculations that have been introduced risen up out of a string of research that developed to an enormous degree freely from the more extensive ADP writing which incorporates, for instance, work under the appearance of "neuro-dynamic programming," "fortification learning," and "HDP."

There are various thoughts in like manner between the calculation that have been introduced and those proposed in this ADP writing. In this segment, one talk about these similitude's and furthermore some striking contrasts.

Like calculations from the more extensive approximate dynamic writing, the calculation approximates a dynamic programming esteem work for use in dynamic. Another striking shared trait is the utilization of recreated state directions and stochastic guess refreshes.

In this regard, the calculation is firmly identified with transient contrast learning, Q-learning Some work in the fortification learning writing features the significance of recreated state directions toward diminishing estimate error.

Maybe this wonder has likewise added to the experimental accomplishment in transportation of calculations. The plan of dynamic projects around the pre-choice state is the most standard treatment in reading material, however, even Bellman's unique treatment of dynamic programming remembered a case of a dynamic programming recursion for terms of a post-choice state.

In the specific situation, such a reformulation of the dynamic programming recursion gets important to empower calculation of fair gauges of the correct hand side by means of reenactment. Such a reformulation is utilized for a similar explanation by Q-learning and SARSA.

One fascinating contrast, however, is that the post-choice state utilized by Q-learning and SARSA is made to be the state-move pair-in a specific situation, this would be (R_t, X_t). The calculation one has introduced, utilizes a progressively miserly representation $R_f = R_t + A_t X_t$ of the post-choice state.

This is conceivable in light of extraordinary structure related with the concern definition, which makes R_f an adequate measurement for foreseeing future commitment. Since Q-learning is intended for progressively broad Markov choice procedures that don't display such structure, it cannot utilize such an adequate measurement.Using a strict adequate measurement has likewise been proposed in a use of ADP to stock administration. The utilization of the post-choice state variable is certain in crafted for a stochastic armada the board issue, and is unequivocal for a similar issue class, and in other issue classes.

Another huge distinction in the calculation is that the updates adjust the subsidiary of the worth capacity regarding state, while most calculations in the ADP writing adjust the qualities themselves.

Plainly, it is the subsidiary of the worth capacity that issues with regards to dynamic, since the worth capacity is just used to look at relative qualities among states. A fascinating issue to investigate might be whether there are basic favorable circumstances to adjusting subordinates instead of qualities.

Despite the fact that adjusting subsidiaries has not been a focal point of the ADP writing, it has gotten some consideration. For instance, this thought has been advanced by Werbos, who proposed various calculations considering this target. This methodology has been effectively applied to issues including a huge number of choice factors.

In spite of the fact that there is some work in the ADP writing on approaches for managing high-dimensional choice spaces, as far as anyone is concerned, no different utilizations of ADP have managed such huge quantities of choice factors.

The utilization of divisible straight and sunken approximations encourages the utilization of whole number programming techniques to upgrade choices.

Despite the fact that distinguishable approximators have been utilized routinely in the ADP writing, there has not been an act of limiting to straight or curved capacities, and their utilization has not been inspired by a need to structure the choice improvement issue.

The distinct straight or inward structure is significant, if increasingly broad nonlinear approximations were utilized this would almost certainly crush integrality properties of fundamental direct projects.

The outcome would be a choice enhancement issue that could not be taken care of adequately by number programming techniques. At last, it is significant that the size of issues handled by the principal creator and partners far surpasses most different uses of ADP announced in the writing.

Specifically, there are commonly a huge number of state factors and a great many choice factors. For issues of such tremendous scope, it gets imperative to utilize techniques for which figure time and memory prerequisites develop gradually with the quantity of state factors.

In this regard, distinct estimation designs are invaluable in light of the fact that the quantity of parameters included develops straightly in the quantity of state factors.

8.10. CONCLUSION

The chapter efficiently describes the approximate dynamic programming concepts and factors related to the computer programming. Aspects of approximate dynamic programming such as sampling strategies, modeling program, etc.

ADP is a most essential procedure to solve huge scope discrete time multistage stochastic control forms, i.e., complex Markov Decision Processes (MDPs). These procedures comprise of a state space S, and at each time step t, the framework is very specific.

Systematic examinations of the impacts of the approximation errors on the nature of the by product of estimated dynamic writing computer programs were directed. It was seen through undisputable presumptions and conditions that the learning results stay limited.

When the learning is ended after a limited number of emphases, it was indicated that the dependability of the outcome can be confirmed, and an estimation of the area of fascination can be obtained. The widespread numerical study of the theoretical outcomes through a nontrivial request issue exhibited the way toward applying the hypothesis.

Given the hypothetical examinations without disregarding the approximation errors and thinking about the end of learning after a limited number of cycles, these results add to the scientific outcomes of ADP.

REFERENCES

1. De Farias, D. P., & Van, R. B., (2003). The linear programming approach to approximate dynamic programming. *Operations Research*, *51*(6), 850–865.
2. Heydari, A., (2016). Theoretical and numerical analysis of approximate dynamic programming with approximation errors. *Journal of Guidance, Control, and Dynamics*, *39*(2), 301–311.
3. Powell, W. B., (2007). *Approximate Dynamic Programming: Solving the Curses of Dimensionality* (Vol. 703). John Wiley & Sons.
4. Si, J., Barto, A. G., Powell, W. B., & Wunsch, D., (2004). *Handbook of Learning and Approximate Dynamic Programming* (Vol. 2). John Wiley & Sons.
5. Villaverde, J., (n.d). *Numerical Dynamic Programming*. [online] Sas.upenn.edu. Available at: https://www.sas.upenn.edu/~jesusfv/lecturetechnical2_numerical_dynamic_programming.pdf (accessed on 4 June 2020).

INDEX